The Origin, Nature, & Destiny of the Soul

Fairland Christian Church
Washington & Mulberry Sts.
835-2984
SS - 9:30am   Worship - 10:30am

Bert Thompson, Ph.D.

APOLOGETICS PRESS

Apologetics Press, Inc.
230 Landmark Drive
Montgomery, Alabama 36117-2752

TABLE OF CONTENTS

ACKNOWLEDGMENTS

I would like to express my gratitude to the following men for their assistance in the preparation of the material contained in this book: Dr. Hugo McCord, professor emeritus of biblical languages, Oklahoma Christianity University of Science and Arts; Dr. William Woodson, professor emeritus and former chairman of the graduate program in Bible, Freed-Hardeman University; and the late Bobby Duncan, former minister of the Church of Christ in Adamsville, Alabama. The suggestions and corrections they offered for incorporation into the finished manuscript were invaluable. The conclusions, however, remain the sole responsibility of the author.

1

INTRODUCTION—SOUL
AND SPIRIT IN SCRIPTURE

Throughout the whole of human history, man has struggled to find answers to any number of important (yet often difficult) questions that have to do with his origin, existence, nature, and destiny. Such queries as "Whence have I come?," "Why am I here?," and "Where am I going?" routinely intrigue and enthrall each of us. Securing clues to the exact makeup of the creature known popularly as *Homo sapiens* always has been one of mankind's keenest intellectual pursuits. And along the way, perhaps no single topic has perplexed us, or piqued our interest, as much as that pertaining to the origin, nature, and destiny of the soul.

Contemplate, if you will, the concept of the soul and the issues that spring from it. What is the definition of a soul? If the soul actually exists, what is its origin? Do humans possess a soul? Do animals? If souls do, in fact, exist, are they purely temporal—thus living only as long as our corporeal nature exists? Or are they immortal—surviving the death of the physical body? What is the difference, if any, between the "soul" and the "spirit"? What is the ultimate destiny of the soul? And what part does the soul play in the biblical statement that men and women were created "in the image of God" (Genesis 1:27)? These are the kinds of issues that I would like to investigate in this book.

The subject of the soul—including its origin, nature, and destiny—has long been controversial. Some people believe that there is no such thing as a soul. Certain individuals advocate the position that only humans possess a soul, but that it ceases to exist at the death of the body. Others seek to maintain that both humans and animals possess a soul, and that those souls likewise die when the physical body dies. Still others are convinced that both animals and humans possess an immortal soul. And finally, there are those who have concluded that humans possess an immortal soul, but that animals do not. What, then, is the truth of the matter?

Science certainly cannot provide the answers to such questions, for they lie far beyond the purview of the scientific method. In her best-selling book, *The Fire in the Equations*, award-winning science writer Kitty Ferguson addressed this very issue. While discussing the efforts of several renowned, modern-day scientists (like eminent physicists Stephen Hawking, Paul Davies, and others) to uncover what they view as a grand, unified "Theory of Everything," she asked:

> Is there anything else? We needn't get spooky about it. Part of the "anything else" might be human minds and personalities. Can we entirely account for our self-awareness, our minds, personalities, intuitions, and emotions, by means of a physical explanation? This is a matter of enormous significance for many of the questions we are asking in this book, and we will return to it frequently. If we are super-complex computing machines—the sum of our physical parts and their mechanical workings, which in turn exist as a result of the process of evolution—then science may ultimately be able to tell us everything there is to know about us. Even if no computer can ever assimilate the human mind, science may find another complete physical explanation. But **we have at present no scientific reason to rule out the possibility that there is more to self-awareness, our minds, and our**

personalities than any such explanation can encompass. Is there such a thing as the soul? If there is, does its existence begin and end with our material existence? Despite some impressive advances in the field of artificial intelligence, and an increasing understanding of the way our minds work, certainly no-one would claim to be able to say at present, except on faith, whether science will eventually be able to assimilate the phenomena of self-awareness, mind, and personality into the materialistic picture. **If science can't, then there is truth beyond the range of scientific explanation.**

Another part of the "anything else" may be what we call the supernatural. Perhaps it is simply figments of imagination, psychological events, not so much to be explained by science as to be explained away. Or perhaps these are real events which are at present unexplainable because we lack complete understanding of the full potential of the physical world. If either is the case, then the supernatural ought eventually to fall into the realm of scientific explanation. However, **if the supernatural world exists**, and if it is inherently beyond testing by the scientific method, **then there is truth beyond the range of scientific explanation**. There may indeed be more in heaven and earth than is dreamed of in our science (if not our philosophy) [1994, pp. 82-83, emp. added].

I would like to seize upon Ferguson's "if...then" proposition as I begin this examination of the origin, nature, and destiny of the soul. Her argument—one that far too few scientists (or science writers) are even willing to consider—is that **if** the supernatural exists, **then** there is truth beyond the range of scientific explanation. The available evidence **does** establish, in fact, that the supernatural exists and that there **is** "truth beyond the range of scientific explanation." As famed NASA astrophysicist (and self-proclaimed agnostic) Robert Jastrow put it: "That there are what I or anyone would call supernatural forces at work, is now, I think, a scientifically proven fact" (1982, p. 18). While I will not present such evidence in this book, I have done so elsewhere in a rather extensive fashion (see, for example, Thompson, 1995a, 1995b, Thompson and Jackson, 1982,

1992). The existence of the supernatural (i.e., God) may be doubted by some and ridiculed by still others, but that does not alter the evidence that establishes its reality.

Thus, whenever questions of spiritual importance are under consideration—as they are when discussing the existence, origin, nature, and destiny of the soul—the only reliable source of information must by necessity be the One Who is the Originator and Sustainer of the soul. God, as Creator of all things physical and spiritual (Genesis 1:1ff., Exodus 20:11), and Himself a Spirit Being (John 4:24), is the ultimate wellspring of the soul. The Bible, then, as God's inspired Word (2 Timothy 3:16-17; 2 Peter 1:20-21), must remain the preeminent authority on this subject. In the great long ago, the psalmist wrote: "The sum of thy word is truth; and every one of thy righteous ordinances endure forever" (119:160). Speaking as a member of the Godhead, Christ said: "Sanctify them in truth; thy word is truth" (John 17:17).

We—if we would know the truth about the soul—must examine that Word in an in-depth fashion and be prepared to accept what it says. Only then can we obtain the answers to the many questions on this vital topic that have perplexed and plagued us through the millennia.

DEFINITION OF THE SOUL

If you and I were in the midst of a conversation and I mentioned the word "banana," likely you would have absolutely no difficulty understanding my meaning. Your thought processes immediately would conjure up a long fruit—with a yellow outer covering and a light beige, inner soft body—that grows on trees and is useful as food for both humans and animals. But were I to ask you to define the term "foil," without seeing the word in context you could not possibly know what I meant. I might be referring to: (1) a noun used to define a fencing sword; (2) a noun that indicates a thin, shiny metal used by cooks in kitchens all over the world; or (3) a verb used as a synonym for "defeat." However, if I were to say, "I covered the turkey with foil prior to placing it in the oven," you would know immediately what I had in mind.

The same is true of the definition of the word "soul." Minus its context, it is difficult, if not impossible, to define accurately. Speaking from the vantage point of a language scholar who had studied the Hebrew and Greek texts for over sixty years, the late Guy N. Woods once suggested that "...there is no pat and easy answer to the question, 'What is the soul?' " (1980, 122[6]:163). Why is this the case? First, the word "soul" in modern English usage is represented by various words in the Hebrew and Greek languages in which the Bible originally was written. Second, those Hebrew and Greek words can have a number of different meanings in their original contexts. Robert Morey has noted:

> These terms are not technical words in the sense that they have one consistent meaning throughout Scripture. They display unity and diversity by being synonymous at times when referring to the immaterial side of man, and at other times, referring to different functions or ways of relating. It is obvious that we should not impose 20th-century standards of consistency and linguistic preciseness to a book which was written thousands of years ago... (1984, p. 44).

Third, the matter of the progressive nature of God's revelation to man must be considered. While it certainly is true that the Lord possesses a constant, unchanging nature (Malachi 3:6; James 1:17), His revelation of that nature and His will for mankind was a progressive process that was adapted to man as he matured spiritually through the ages. This explains why, in the course of human history, God sometimes tolerated in man both attitudes and actions that were less than what the divine ideal intended. This, of course, does not mean that the Holy God vacillates in His ethics or morality; rather, it simply means that—because of His infinite love—He dealt gently and compassionately with man in the particular state of spiritual maturation in which He found him at the time (cf. Acts

14:15-16 and 17:30-31). As God progressively revealed more and more of both His nature and His will, He did so in a manner, and in terms, that fit the occasion. In addressing the failure of some to comprehend and appreciate the importance of this concept, Morey observed that certain words, therefore,

> ...may have a dozen different meanings, **depending on the context and the progressive nature of revelation**. The failure to avoid reductionistic and simplistic definitions is based on the hidden assumption that once the meaning of a word is discovered in a single passage, this same meaning must prevail in every other occurrence of the word.... The resistance to the idea that what soul meant to Moses was probably not what it meant to David or Paul is based on their unconscious assumption that the Bible is one book written at one time. Thus as we approach the biblical term which describes the immaterial side of man, we will not attempt to develop artificial definitions based upon the absolutizing of the meaning of a word in a single passage but recognize that a contextual approach will reveal a wide range of meanings (1984, pp. 44-45, emp. added).

The word "soul" does indeed enjoy a "wide range of meanings." In order to understand those meanings, it is necessary to examine how the word is employed within the various contexts in Scripture where it appears.

Use of the Word "Soul" in Scripture

The word for "soul" in the Bible (Hebrew *nephesh* [from *naphash*, to breathe]; Greek *psuche*) is used in at least four different ways (see Arndt and Gingrich, 1957, pp. 901-902; Thayer, 1958, p. 677). First, the term is employed simply as a synonym for a person. Moses wrote: "All the souls (*nephesh*) that came out of the loins of Jacob were seventy souls (*nephesh*)" (Exodus 1:5; cf. Deuteronomy 10:22). In legal matters, the word soul often was used to denote an individual. The Lord told Moses: "Speak unto the children of Israel, saying, 'If a soul (*nephesh*) shall sin through ignorance against any of the commandments of the Lord concerning things which ought not to be done'..." (Leviticus 4:2). When Jacob was speaking of himself in Genesis 49:6, he used the expression, "O my soul (*nephesh*)"—which meant simply "me." Numbers 9:6 records that "there were certain men, who were unclean by reason of the dead body (*nephesh meth*) of a man, so that they could not keep the Passover on that day" (cf. Number 6:6 and Ecclesiastes 9:5). In the New Testament, the word *psuche* is employed in the same manner. In Acts 2:41, Luke recorded that "there were added unto them in that day about three thousand souls (*psuchai*)." In Peter's first epistle, when he addressed the topic of the Genesis Flood he referred to the fact that "few, that is eight souls (*psuchai*), were saved by water" (3:20). In each of these instances, actual people—individually or collectively—were under discussion.

Second, the word soul is used to denote the form of life that man possesses in common with animals and that ceases to exist at death. In their widely used *Hebrew and English Lexicon of the Old Testament*, Brown, Driver, and Briggs noted that *nephesh* often is employed to mean "life principle" (1907, p. 659). In the King James Version, *nephesh* is translated as "soul" in the Old Testament 472 times, as "life" 118 times, and as "creature" 8 times; *psuche* is translated as "soul" in the New Testament 59 times and as "life" 39 times (Morey, 1984, pp. 45,55). In addressing the use of the word "soul" in such passages as Genesis 2:7 and 1:20, Woods wrote:

> ...the word **soul** from the Hebrew *nephesh* occurs, for the first time in the sacred writings, at Genesis 1:20, where it is assigned to fish, birds, and creeping things. (See also, another similar usage in Genesis 1:30.) As thus used, it is clear that the soul in these passages does not refer to anything peculiar to the constitution of man. It signifies, as its usage denotes, and the lexicons affirm, **any creature that breathes**, in all of these early occurrences in the book of Genesis. Nor is it correct to conclude that the phrase **breath of life** in the

statement of Moses ("And the Lord God formed man of the dust of the ground, and breathed into his nostrils the breath of life; and man became a living soul") sums up, or was designed to denote the **whole** constitution of man. The word "life" here is, in the Hebrew text, plural, literally **breath of lives** (*nishmath khay-yim*). It occurs, in similar form, in three other instances in the early chapters of Genesis (6:17; 7:15; 7:22). In the first of these the phrase is *ruach khay-yim*; in the second the same; in the third, *nishmath-ruach khay-yim*, and out of the four instances where the phrase, the **breath of lives**, occurs in our translation the last three are applied to the beasts, birds and creeping things. It follows, therefore, that the phrase "breath of life" does not designate anything peculiar to man. And in view of the fact that the word "soul," from the Hebrew *nephesh*, is similarly extended to include the animal world, birds and creeping things, it may not be properly limited to man... (1985, 127 [22]:691, emp. and parenthetical comment in orig.).

In Genesis 1:20,24, and 30, God spoke of the *nephesh hayyah*—literally "soul breathers" or "life breathers" (often translated as "living creatures" or "life"—cf. Leviticus 11:10; grammatically the phrase is singular but it bears a plural meaning). The writer of Proverbs stated in regard to animals: "A righteous man regardeth the life (*nephesh*) of his beast; But the tender mercies of the wicked are cruel" (12:10). Hebrew scholar Hugo McCord therefore noted:

Then the translators realized that the first meaning of *nephesh* is "breath," and so Genesis 1:20,24,30 and Genesis 2:7 all fit together in understanding Moses as saying that all animals and man too are breathers. Breathers, coupled with *hayyah*, "living," the translators thought, would be well translated, in the case of animals, as "living creatures," and in the case of man as a "living being" (1995, 23[1]:87-88).

In Exodus 21:23, Moses commanded: "But if any harm follow, then thou shalt give life (*nephesh*) for life (*nephesh*)." He later wrote that "the life (*nephesh*) of the flesh is in the blood" (Leviticus 17:11, 14). Blood often is said to be the seat of life because when blood is shed, death ensues (cf. Deuteronomy 12:23). In speaking of God's retribution upon the Egyptians during the time of the Exodus, the psalmist wrote: "He spared not their soul (*nephesh*) from death, but gave their life over to the pestilence" (78:50). In this particular instance, the Egyptians' souls represented their physical life and nothing more. Ezekiel later observed: "The soul (*nephesh*) that sinneth, it shall die" (18:20).

In the New Testament, the principle is the same. Christ observed in regard to humans: "Therefore I say unto you, be not anxious for your life (*psuche*), what ye shall eat, or what ye shall drink; nor yet for your body" (Matthew 6:25). God told Joseph: "Arise and take the young child and his mother, and go into the land of Israel: for they are dead that sought the young child's life" (*psuche*, Matthew 2:19). In the book of Revelation, John spoke of the fact that "there died the third part of the creatures which were in the sea, even they that had life (*psuchas*); and the third part of the ships was destroyed" (8:9; cf. 16:3, *psuche*). Many a follower of Christ was said to have risked his or her life (*psuche*) for the Lord. In Acts 15:25-26, Luke recorded that Barnabas and Paul were "men that have hazarded their lives (*psuchas*) for the name of our Lord Jesus Christ." Earlier, John recorded Peter as saying to the Lord: "I will lay down my life (*psuchen*) for thee" (John 13:37-38). In Philippians 2:30ff., Paul spoke of "Epaphroditus, my brother and fellow-worker and fellow-soldier...hazarding his life (*psuche*) to supply that which was lacking in your service toward me." And in Luke 14:26, one of the conditions of discipleship was to hate one's own life (*psuche*)—that is, to be willing to deny oneself to the point of losing one's life for Christ (cf. Luke 9:23; Revelation 12:11).

Third, the idea of the soul is used to refer to the varied emotions or inner thoughts of a man—a fact that explains why *nephesh* is translated "heart" (15 times) or "mind" (15 times) in the Old Testament (KJV) and why *psuche* is translated as "heart" (1 time) and "mind" (3 times) in the New. Man was called to love God with all his heart and with all his soul (*nephesh*; Deuteronomy 13:3b). The soul (*nephesh*) is said to weep (Job 30:16; Psalm 119:28) and to be exercised in patience (Job 6:7-11). From the soul (*nephesh*) originate knowledge and understanding (Psalm 139:14), thought (1 Samuel 20:3), love (1 Samuel 18:1), and memory (Lamentations 3:20). In His discussion with a lawyer, Jesus said: "Thou shalt love the Lord thy God with all thy heart, and with all thy soul (*psuche*), and with all thy mind" (Matthew 22:37). In Acts 4:32, Luke recorded how, on one occasion, "the multitude of them that believed were of one heart and soul (*psuche*)." In a similar fashion, "soul" also is employed to refer to the lower, physical nature of mankind. In his first letter to the Christians at Corinth, Paul wrote that "the **natural man** receiveth not the things of the Spirit of God" (2:14). In addressing the specific intent of this passage, Woods noted that the phrase "natural man" is literally

> **the soulish man**, since the adjective "natural" [*psuchikos*— BT] translates a form of the Greek word for soul, which may be expressed in English as **psychical**. Thus, this usage is supported by etymology and required by the context. See, especially, Paul's teaching in 1 Corinthians 1:18-28 and 2:6-16 (1980, 122[6]:163, emp. in orig.).

Fourth, the word soul is used in Scripture to designate the portion of a person that is immortal and thus never dies. As early as the book of Genesis, the Bible sets forth such a concept. For example, in commenting on Rachel's untimely death at the birth of her son, Moses wrote: "And it came to pass, as her soul (*nephesh*) was departing (for she died), that she called his name Ben-oni: but his father called him Benjamin" (Genesis 35:18). On one occasion while the prophet Elijah was at the house of a widow in the city of Zarephath, the woman's son fell ill and eventually died. But the text indicates that Elijah "cried unto Jehovah..., 'O Jehovah my God, I pray thee, let this child's soul (*nephesh*) come into him again'" (1 Kings 17:21). When the psalmist prayed to Jehovah for forgiveness, he cried: "O Jehovah, have mercy upon me: heal my soul (*nephesh*); for I have sinned against thee" (41:4). In his discussion of the ultimate fate of those who dared to trust in earthly riches rather than in the supreme power of the God of heaven, the psalmist lamented that such people were "like the beasts that perish.... But God will redeem my soul (*nephesh*) from the power of Sheol" (49:15).

Many years later, Christ warned His disciples: "And be not afraid of them that kill the body, but are not able to kill the soul: but rather fear him who is able to destroy both soul (*psuche*) and body in hell" (Matthew 10:28). During His discussion with the Sadducees in Matthew 22, the Lord quoted from Exodus 3:6 where God said to Moses: "I **am** the God of Abraham, and the God of Isaac, and the God of Jacob." Christ then went on to state (22:32): "God is not the God of the dead, but of the living"—a fact that the Sadducees' opponents, the Pharisees, already accepted as true (cf. Acts 23:8). Yet when God spoke with Moses (c. 1446 B.C.) about the patriarchs Abraham, Isaac, and Jacob, those three men had been dead and in their tombs for literally hundreds of years.

Since from Christ's own words we know that "God is not the God of the dead, but of the living," the point is obvious. Abraham, Isaac, and Jacob still must have been living. But how? The solution to the seeming problem, of course, lies in the fact that while their **bodies** had died, their immortal **souls** had not. When the apostle John was allowed to peer into the book "sealed with seven seals" (Revelation 5:1), he "saw underneath the altar the souls (*psuchas*) of them that had been slain for the word of God" (Revelation 6:9). Each of these passages is instructive of the fact that there is within man a soul that never dies.

Use of the Word "Spirit" in Scripture

During his tenure as associate editor of the *Gospel Advocate*, Guy N. Woods penned a "Questions and Answers" column in which he dealt with difficult Bible questions, topics, or passages. When one querist wrote to ask: "What is the difference between the soul and the spirit of man?," Woods responded as follows:

Though it is characteristic of most people today to use these terms interchangeably the scriptures very definitely differentiate them. "For the word of God is living, and active, and sharper than any two-edged sword, and piercing even to the dividing of **soul** and **spirit**, of both joints and marrow, and quick to discern the thoughts and intents of the heart." (Hebrews 4:12.) Since the sacred writers provided for "the dividing of soul and spirit," in those instances where they differ, so ought we and so we must if we are to entertain biblical concepts of these words.

The word "spirit," when denoting the human entity (from the Greek word *pneuma*), is a specific term and designates that part of us which is not susceptible to death and which survives the dissolution of the body. (Acts 7:59.) It is infused in us directly from God and is not a product of human generation. (Hebrews 12:9.) "Soul," from the Greek word *psuche*, however, is a generic word and its meaning must be determined, in any given instance, from the context in which it appears (1980, 122[6]:163, emp. added).

In my above discussion on the use of the word "soul" in Scripture, I examined the various ways in which the Hebrew and Greek terms for soul are employed. I now would like to examine the various ways in which the Hebrew and Greek terms for "spirit" are employed within the sacred text.

The Hebrew term for "spirit" is *ruach* (from *rawah*, to breathe). In their *Hebrew and English Lexicon of the Old Testament*, Brown, Driver, and Briggs noted that *ruach* has nine different meanings, depending on the specific context. *Ruach* may refer to:(1) the Holy Spirit; (2) angels, both good and evil; (3) the life principle found within both man and animals; (4) disembodied spirits; (5) breath; (6) wind; (7) disposition or attitude; (8) the seat of emotions; and (9) the seat of mind and will in men (1907, pp. 924-925). In the Old Testament of the King James Version, *ruach* is translated variously as the Spirit of God (i.e., Holy Spirit) 105 times, man's spirit 59 times, spirit (an attitude or emotional state) 51 times, spirits (angels) 23 times, wind 43 times, and several other items (Morey, 1984, p. 51).

The word *ruach*, like *nephesh*, has a wide range of meanings. First, it seems originally to have referred to the wind, which was viewed as being invisible and immaterial (Gen. 8: 1). Second, since God is invisible and immaterial like the wind, He is described as "spirit" (Isa. 63:10). Third, since the angels of God are invisible and immaterial, they are called "spirits" (Ps. 104:4, KJV; cf. Heb. 1:14). Fourth, since the life principle which animates man and animals is invisible and immaterial, it is also called "spirit" (Gen. 7:22). In this sense it was viewed as the "breath" of life which departs at death. Fifth, since man has an invisible and immaterial self or soul which transcends the life principle by its self-consciousness, man's "mind" or "heart" is called his "spirit" (Ps. 77:6; Prov. 29:11, KJV). The invisible side of man which is called "spirit" cannot be reduced to the mere principle of physical life or the breath of the body because man's transcendent self is contrasted to those things in such places as Isa. 42:5. Also, man's self-awareness as a cognitive ego obviously transcends the life principle which operates in animals. At death, this transcendent ego or disincarnate mind is called a "spirit" or a "ghost" (Job 4:15). This is parallel to *rephaim* or disembodied spirit (Job 26:5). Thus at death, while the life principle or breath of life ceases to exist in man or animals, the higher self or spirit of man ascends at death to the presence of God (Ps. 31:5; Eccles. 12: 7).... Sixth, since attitudes and dispositions such as pride, humility, joy, or sorrow are invisible and immaterial, they are described as being someone's "spirit" (Prov. 11:13; 16:18). The Holy Spirit is described as the "sevenfold Spirit" in the sense that He gives people the disposition, attitude, or spirit of wisdom, understanding, counsel, might, knowledge, fear and holiness (Isa. 11:2; cf. Rom. 1:4; Rev. 3:1) [Morey, 1984, pp. 52-53].

The Greek term for "spirit" is *pneuma* (from *pneo*, to breathe). In their *Greek-English Lexicon of the New Testament and Other Early Christian Literature*, language scholars Arndt and Gingrich noted that *pneuma* has seven different meanings, depending on the specific context. *Pneuma* may refer to: (1) wind or air; (2) that which gives life to the body; (3) disincarnate souls; (4) human personality or ego which is the center of emotion, intellect, and will; (5) a state of mind or disposition; (6) an independent, immaterial being such as God or angels; and (7) as God—as in the Holy Spirit of God, the spirit of Christ, etc. (1957, pp. 680-685). In his *Greek-English Lexicon of the New Testament,* Thayer provided five definitions for *pneuma* (1958, pp. 520-524). In the King James Version of the New Testament, *pneuma* is translated variously as Spirit (Holy) 165 times, Ghost (Holy) 88 times, spirits (good/evil, angels) 55 times, spirit (man's) 45 times, spirit (attitude) 22 times, spirits or ghosts (man's disincarnate soul) 7 times, spiritual (adjectival use) 23 times, life and wind 1 time each (Morey, pp. 60-61).

> The word *pneuma* in its various forms is found 406 times in the New Testament.... First, the New Testament writers carry on the precedent set by the translators of the Septuagint by using the Greek words for wind such as *animas* instead of *pneuma.* The only instance where *pneuma* definitely refers to the wind is in John 3:8 where there is a poetic play upon the sovereign movement of the divine Spirit and the wind. Second, *pneuma* refers to the life principle which animates the body. This is actually a very rare usage in the New Testament. For example, the false prophet who accompanied the Antichrist in the last days will make an idol "alive" (Rev. 13:15). Third, *pneuma* is used to describe the immaterial nature of God and angels (John 4:24; Heb. 1:14). Christ defined a "spirit" or "ghost" as an immaterial being (Luke 24:39). Fourth, *pneuma* refers to the disposition which characterizes a person, such as pride, humility, fear, etc. (1 Pet. 3:4). Fifth, *pneuma* is used to describe the disincarnate spirit or soul of man after death (Matt. 27:50; Luke 24:37,39; John 19:30; Acts 7:59; Heb. 12:23; 1 Pet. 3:19).... Sixth, man's transcendent self, or ego, is also called *pneuma* because of its immaterial and invisible nature (1 Cor. 2:11). It is described as the center of man's emotions, intellect and will (Mark 8:12; Mark 2:8; Matt. 26:41). Since man's *pneuma* transcends his mere physical life, it is frequently contrasted to his body, or flesh (Matt. 26:41; Mark 14:38; Luke 24:39; John 3:6; 6:63; 1 Cor.

5:5; 7:34; 2 Cor. 7:1; Gal. 5:17; 6:8,9; James 2:26). It is man's *pneuma* which ascends to God at death (Acts 7:59) [Morey, pp. 61-62].

Since *ruach* and *pneuma* both derive from roots meaning "to breathe," it should not be surprising that on occasion they are used synonymously, as the information in Table 1 documents.

SPIRIT	REFERS TO	SOUL
Genesis 6:17; 7:15; Ecclesiastes 3:19	Breath	Job 41:21
Genesis 7:22	Animal/Human Life	Genesis 9:4; 37:21 Matthew 2:20; 6:25
Ecclesiastes 12:7; 1 Corinthians 5:5	Entities Separate from the Body	Isaiah 10:18; Matthew 10:28
Mark 2:8; 1 Corinthians 2:11; 14:15	Seat of Man's Intellect	Hebrews 12:3; Philippians 1:27
Genesis 41:8; Proverbs 16:18; 17:22; Mark 8:12; Acts 18:25; 1 Corinthians 4:21; 2 Corinthians 2:13	Feelings and Emotions	Exodus 23:9; Psalm 42:1-6; Proverbs 12:10; Matthew 26:38; Luke 2:35; Acts 4:32; 17:16; 2 Peter 2:8
Genesis 1:2; 6:3; Matthew 12:18; John 4:24	God's Nature	Leviticus 26:11; Matthew 12:18; Hebrews 10:38
Psalm 51:10,17; Luke 1:46-47; John 4:24; Romans 1:9	Man's Place of Inner Worship and Reverence Toward God	Psalms 42:1-2,4-6; 103:1; 146:1; Matthew 22:37
Psalm 31:5; Ecclesiastes 12:7; Zechariah 12:1; Luke 8:55; 23:46; Acts 7:59; 1 Corinthians 5:5	Part of a Person that Lives on after Death of the Body	Genesis 35:18; 1 Kings 17:21-22; Psalms 41:4; 49:15; Micah 6:7; Matthew 10:28; Hebrews 10:39; James 1:21; 5:20; 1 Peter 1:9,22; 3 John 2; Revelation 6:9

Table 1. Synonymous Use of Spirit/Soul in the Old and New Testaments

Writing in the *International Standard Bible Encyclopedia* about both the similarities and the differences between the Old Testament words *nephesh* and *ruach* as compared to their New Testament counterparts *psuche* and *pneuma*, J.I. Marais noted:

> In the NT *psuche* appears under more or less similar conditions as in the OT. The contrast here is as carefully maintained as there. It is used where *pneuma* would be out of place; and yet it seems at times to be employed where *pneuma* might have been substituted. Thus in Jn. 19:30 we read: "Jesus gave up His *pneuma* to the Father," and, in the same Gospel (Jn. 10:15), "Jesus gave up His *psuche* for the sheep," and in Mt. 20:28 He gave His *psuche* (not His *pneuma*) as a ransom... (1956, 5:2838).

While the "spirit" (*pneuma*) is recognized as man's individual possession (i.e., that which distinguishes one man from another and from inanimate nature), on occasion the same may be said of the soul (*psuche*; cf. Matthew 10:28 and Revelation 6:9-11). The *pneuma* of Christ was surrendered to the Father in death; His *psuche* was surrendered, His individual life was given, "a ransom for many." His life "was given for the sheep." In Acts 2:27, Luke quoted Psalm 16:10 regarding Christ's physical death: "Because thou wilt not leave my soul unto hades, neither wilt thou give thy Holy One to see corruption." The word that Luke used for "soul" is *psuche*, which is employed here not only as the Greek counterpart to the Hebrew *nephesh*, meaning body, but representing specifically a *nephesh meth*— a dead body (cf. Numbers 6:6, 9:6, and Ecclesiastes 9:5). Thus, Christ's body was not abandoned to hades.

Hades is used in Scripture to refer to at least three different places: (a) the general abode of the spirits of the dead, whether good or evil (Revelation 1:18; 6:8; 20:13-14); (b) a temporary place of punishment for the wicked dead (Luke 16:23; Revelation 20:13); and (c) the grave (1 Corinthians 15:55; cf. Acts 2:27). In Psalm 16:10 (the passage quoted by Luke in Acts 2:27), the writer stated: "Thou wilt not leave my soul (*nephesh*) to sheol." In the Old Testament, sheol also is used to refer to three different places: (a) the unseen abode for spirits of the dead (Job 14:13-15; Ezekiel 26:20; Jonah 2:2); (b) a temporary place of punishment for the wicked dead (Psalm 9:17); and (c) the grave (Davidson, 1970, p. 694; Harris, et al., 1980, 2:892; cf. Numbers 16:30-37 where the conclusion of the rebellion of Korah [and those sympathetic with him] against Moses is described in these words: "The earth opened its mouth, and swallowed them up, and their households, and all the men that appertained unto Korah, and all their goods. So they, and all that appertained to them, went down alive into sheol."). In Acts 2:27 (hades) and Psalm 16:10 (sheol), the context seems to require the latter usage—i.e., the grave. Thus, both David and Luke were making the point (to paraphrase): "You will not leave my body in the grave, nor will you allow your Holy One to see decay." In fact, just four verses later, the inspired writer referred back to David's declaration and commented that "he foreseeing this spake of the resurrection of the Christ, that neither was he left unto hades, nor did his flesh see corruption" (2:31).

In referring to the death of the physical body, Solomon wrote that "the living know that they shall die: but the dead know not anything" (Ecclesiastes 9:5). The psalmist addressed the same point when he wrote: "The dead praise not Jehovah, Neither any that go down into silence" (115:17) and "His breath goeth forth, he returneth to his earth; in that very day his thoughts perish" (146:4). When Christ yielded up His soul/life (*psuche*; cf. *nephesh*, Psalm 16:10), His dead body was headed for the grave and therefore was in the condition that it could "know not anything" and "praise not Jehovah." [The spirit (*pneuma*) that had vacated the body was alive and well in Paradise (Greek *paradeisos*, Luke 23:43). Paul addressed this principle when he said that Christ's disciples always should be "of good courage, and willing rather to be **absent from the body**, and to be **at home with the Lord**" (2 Corinthians 5:8; cf. 1 Thessalonians 4:14).] Woods observed:

> Death, mortality, corruptibility, decay, destruction are never affirmed of the spirit. It is, in the nature of the case, impossible for a spirit to die. The scriptures affirm deathlessness of the angels; and the angels do not die because they are angels, but because they are spirits (1985, 127[22]:692).

Yet it also is impossible for a soul to die (Matthew 10:28; Revelation 6:9-11).

However, as Hebrews 4:12 documents, there are times when the words spirit and soul are **not** used synonymously. The word spirit sometimes refers to wind or air (Genesis 3:8; 8:1; John 3:8); the word soul does not. The word spirit sometimes refers to demons (Mark 5:2; Luke 9:39); the word soul does not. The word soul sometimes refers to both the inner and outer man (i.e., a whole person; Exodus 1:5; Ezekiel 18:20; Acts 2:41; Romans 13:1); the word spirit does not. The word soul sometimes refers to a corpse (Numbers 5:2; 6:6; Psalm 16:10; Acts 2:27); the word spirit does not. The word soul on one occasion refers to an odor, fragrance, or perfume (Isaiah 3:20); the word spirit does not.

Thus, while it is true that on some occasions the words "soul" and "spirit" are used interchangeably, in other instances they are employed in a non-synonymous fashion. As Woods observed, under certain conditions within Scripture "lexically, logically, and actually these terms differ and must not be confused" (1985, 127[22]: 692). In any study of these two terms as they occur within God's Word, the context and intent of the writers are the deciding factors that must be considered and respected.

2

THE ORIGIN AND SOURCE OF THE SOUL

Biblical teaching regarding man acknowledges that he is composed of two distinct parts—the physical and the spiritual. We get an introduction to the origin of the **physical** portion as early as Genesis 2:7 when the text states: "Jehovah God formed man of the dust of the ground, and breathed into his nostrils the breath of life; and man became a living soul (*nephesh chayyah*)." It is important to recognize both what this passage is discussing and what it is not. Genesis 2:7 **is** teaching that man was given **physical life**; it is **not** teaching that man was instilled with an **immortal nature**. The immediate (as well as the remote) context is important to a clear understanding of the intent of Moses' statement. Both the King James and American Standard Versions translate *nephesh chayyah* as "living soul." The Revised Standard Version, New American Standard Version, New International Version, and the New Jerusalem Bible all translate the phrase as "living being." The New English Bible translates it as "living creature."

The variety of terms employed in our English translations has caused some confusion as to the exact meaning of the phrase "living soul" or "living being." Some have suggested, for example, that Genesis 2:7 is speaking specifically of man's receiving his immortal soul and/or spirit. This is not the case, however, as a closer examination of the immediate and remote contexts clearly indicates. For example, the apostle Paul quoted Genesis 2:7 in 1 Corinthians 15:44-45 when he wrote: "If there is a **natural body**, there is also a **spiritual body**. So also it is written, 'The first man Adam became a living soul.' The last Adam became a life-giving spirit." The comparison/contrast offered by the apostle between the first Adam's "natural body" and the last Adam (Christ) as a "life-giving spirit" is absolutely critical to an understanding of Paul's central message (and the theme of the great "resurrection chapter" of the Bible, 1 Corinthians 15), and must not be overlooked in any examination of Moses' statement in Genesis 2:7.

There are six additional places in the Old Testament where similar phraseology is employed, and in each case the text obviously is speaking of members of the animal kingdom. In Genesis 1:24, God said: "Let the earth bring forth living creatures (*nephesh chayyah*) after their kind." Genesis 1:30 records that God provided plants as food "to every beast of the earth, and to every bird of the air, and to everything that creeps on the earth, everything that has the breath of life (*nishmath chayyah*)." When the Genesis Flood covered the Earth, God made a rainbow covenant with Noah and with every living creature (*nephesh chayyah*) that was in the ark with Him (Genesis 9:12). God pledged that He would remember the covenant that He made with every "living creature" (*nephesh chayyah;* Genesis 9:12), and therefore He never again would destroy the Earth by such a Flood. The rainbow, He stated, would serve as a reminder of that "everlasting covenant" between God and every living creature (*nephesh chayyah,* Genesis 9:15). The final occurrence of the phrase is found in Ezekiel's description of the river flowing from the temple in which every living creature (*nephesh chayyah*) that swarms will live (47:9).

Additionally, the Bible declares: "For that which befalleth the sons of men befalleth beasts; even one thing befalleth them: as the one dieth, so dieth the other; yea, they have all one breath; and man hath no preeminence above the beasts" (Ecclesiastes 3:19). Does this mean, therefore, that man possesses only a material nature and has no immortal soul/spirit? No, it does not! In speaking to this very point, Jack P. Lewis wrote:

> It would seem that arguments which try to present the distinctiveness of man from the term "living soul" are actually based on the phenomena of variety in translation of the KJV and have no validity in fact. Had the translators rendered all seven occurrences by the same term, we would have been aware of the fact that both men and animals are described by it. To make this observation is not at all to affirm that the Old Testament is materialistic. We are concerned at this time only with the biblical usage of one term. Neither is it to deny a distinction in biblical thought between men and other animals when one takes in consideration the whole Old Testament view. Man may perish like the animals, but he is different from them. Even here in Genesis in the creation account, God is not said to breathe into the animals the breath of life; animals are made male and female; there is no separate account of the making of the female animal; they are not said to be in God's image and likeness; they are not given dominion. Man is the crown of God's creation (1988, p. 7).

When Dr. Lewis suggested that "man may perish like the animals," he captured the essence of the passage in Ecclesiastes 3:19. It is true that both men and beasts ultimately die, and that in this regard man "hath no preeminence above the beasts." Yet while both creatures are referred to as *nephesh chayyah*, the Scriptures make it clear that God did something special in reference to man. Genesis 1:26-27 records: "And God said, Let us make man **in our image, after our likeness**.... And God created man in his own image, in the image of God created he him; male and female created he them." Nowhere does the Bible state or imply that animals are created in the image of God. What is it, then, that makes man different from the animals?

The answer, of course, lies in the fact that man possesses an immortal nature. Animals do not. God Himself is a spirit (John 4:24). And a spirit "hath not flesh and bones" (Luke 24:39). In some fashion, God has placed within man a portion of His own essence—in the sense that man possesses a spirit that never will die. The prophet Zechariah spoke of Jehovah, Who "stretcheth forth the heavens, and layeth the foundation of the earth, and formeth the spirit (*ruach*) of man within him" (12:1). The Hebrew word for "formeth," *yatsar*, is defined as to form, fashion, or shape (as in a potter working with clay; Harris, et al., 1980, 1:396). The same word is used in Genesis 2:7, thereby indicating that both man's physical body and his spiritual nature were formed, shaped, molded, or fashioned by God. The authors of the *Theological Wordbook of the Old Testament* noted:

> The participial form meaning "potter" is applied to God in Isa. 64:7 where mankind is the work of his hand. When applied to the objects of God's creative work, the emphasis of the word is on the forming or structuring of these phenomena. The word speaks to the **mode of creation** of these phenomena only insofar as the act of shaping or forming an object may also imply the **initiation of that object** (Harris, et al., 1:396, emp. added).

As the Creator, God "initiates" the object we know as man's immortal nature (i.e., his soul or spirit). Solomon, writing in the book of Ecclesiastes, noted that "the dust returneth to the earth as it was, and the spirit returneth unto **God who gave it**" (12:7, emp. added). Man's physical body was formed of the physical dust of the Earth. Would it not follow, then, that his spiritual portion would be formed from that which is spiritual? When the writer of Hebrews referred to God as "the Father of our spirits" (12:9), he revealed the spiritual source of the soul—God.

WHEN DOES MAN RECEIVE HIS IMMORTAL NATURE?

When does man receive his soul/spirit? In one of the most illustrative passages within the Bible on this topic, James wrote: "The body apart from the spirit is dead" (2:26). This brief but important observation—offered by inspiration on the part of the Bible writer —carries tremendous implications. Without the presence of the spirit (*pneuma*), the physical body cannot live. There is, however, an important corollary to James' assessment. If the body is living, **then the spirit (*pneuma*) must be present!**

But when does life actually begin? The answer, quite simply, is that it begins **at conception**. When the male and female gametes join to form the zygote that eventually will grow into the fetus, it is at that very moment that the formation of a new body begins. It is the result of a **viable** male gamete joined sexually with a **viable** female gamete which has formed a zygote that will move through a variety of important stages.

The first step in the process—which eventually will result in the highly differentiated tissues and organs that compose the body of the neonatal child—is the initial mitotic cleavage of that primal cell, the zygote. At this point, the genetic material doubles, matching copies of the chromosomes move to opposite poles, and the cell cleaves into two daughter cells. Shortly afterwards, each of these cells divides again, forming the embryo. [In humans and animals, the term "embryo" applies to any stage after cleavage but before birth (see Rudin, 1997, p. 125).]

As the cells of the embryo continue to divide, they form a cluster of cells. These divisions are accompanied by additional changes that produce a hollow, fluid-filled cavity inside the ball, which now is a one-layer-thick grouping of cells known as a blastula. Early in the second day after fertilization, the embryo undergoes a process known as gastrulation in which the single-layer blastula turns into a three-layered gastrula consisting of ectoderm, mesoderm, and endoderm surrounding a cavity known as the archenteron. Each of these layers will give rise to very specific structures. For example, the ectoderm will form the outermost layer of the skin and other structures, including the sense organs, parts of the skeleton, and the nervous system. The mesoderm will form tissues associated with support, movement, transport, reproduction, and excretion (i.e., muscle, bone, cartilage, blood, heart, blood vessels, gonads, and kidneys). The endo-derm will produce structures associated with breathing and digestion (including the lungs, liver, pancreas, and other digestive glands) [see Wallace, 1975, p. 187].

Within 72 hours after fertilization, the embryo will have divided a total of four times, and will consist of sixteen cells. Each cell will divide before it reaches the size of the cell that produced it; hence, the cells will become progressively smaller with each division. By the end of the first month, the embryo will have reached a length of only one-eighth of an inch, but already will consist of millions of cells. By the end of the ninth month, if all proceeds via normal channels, a baby is ready to be born. As one biologist (and author of a widely used secular university biology textbook) noted: "As soon as the egg is touched by the head of a sperm, it undergoes violent pulsating movements which unite the twenty-three chromosomes of the sperm with its own genetic complement. From this single cell, about 1/175 of an inch in diameter, **a baby** weighing several pounds and composed of trillions of cells will be delivered about 266 days later" (Wallace, 1975, p. 194, emp. added).

Is it alive? Of course it is alive. In fact, herein lies one of the most illogical absurdities of arguments set forth by those who support and defend abortion. They opine that the "thing" in the human womb is not "alive." If it is not alive, why the need to abort it? **Simply leave it alone!** Obviously, of course, from their perspective that is not an option because, as everyone knows, in nine months that growing, vibrant, developing fetus results in a **living human baby**. The truth of the matter is that human life begins at conception and is contin-uous, whether intrauterine or extrauterine, until death. Consider the following scientific facts regarding the living nature of the fetus.

(1) The baby's heart starts beating 18-25 days after con-ception.

(2) By the age of two months, the heart beats so strongly that a doctor actually can listen to it with a special stethoscope.

(3) At about this same time, brain activity can be recorded by use of an electroencephalogram. Brain waves are readily apparent.

(4) By the age of two months, everything is "in place"—feet, hands, head, organs, etc. Upon close examination, fingerprints are evident. Although less than an inch long, the embryo has a head with eyes and ears, a simple digestive system, kidneys, liver, a heart that beats, a bloodstream of its own, and the beginning of a brain.

(5) The unborn child hiccups, sucks his or her thumb, wakes, and sleeps.

(6) The unborn child responds to touch, pain, cold, sound, and light.

Is the child alive? Do you know any **dead** creature that attains such marvelous accomplishments?

But is the fetus growing in the uterus actually **human**? It is the result of the union of the **human** male gamete (spermatozoon) and the **human** female gamete (ovum)—something that certainly guarantees its humanness. [The *Washington Post* of May 11, 1975 contained an "Open Letter to the Supreme Court"—signed by 209 medical doctors—which stated: "We physicians reaffirm our dedication to the awesome splendor of **human life—from one-celled infant to dottering elder**."]

And how, exactly, does God view this unborn yet fully human child? He said to the prophet Jeremiah: "Before I formed thee in the belly, I knew thee, and **before thou camest forth out of the womb**, I sanctified thee" (Jeremiah 1:5, emp. added). Jehovah knew the prophet—even while he was *in utero*—and viewed him as a living person. Further, God already had "sanctified" Jeremiah. If his mother had aborted the baby, she would have killed someone that God recognized as a living person.

The same concept applied to the prophet Isaiah who said: "Listen, O isles, unto me, and hearken ye peoples, from afar; **Jehovah hath called me from the womb**; from the bowels of my mother hath he made mention of my name.... And now, saith Jehovah that **formed me from the womb** to be his servant..." (Isaiah 49:1,5, emp. added). Jehovah not only viewed Isaiah as a person prior to his birth, but even called him by name.

David, writing in Psalm 139:13-16, provided one of the clearest and most compelling discussions on the nature and importance of life *in utero* when he wrote:

> For thou didst form my inward parts: Thou didst cover me in my mother's womb. I will give thanks unto thee; For I am fearfully and wonderfully made: Wonderful are thy works; And that my soul knoweth right well. My frame was not hidden from thee, When I was made in secret, And curiously wrought in the lowest parts of the earth. Thine eyes did see mine unformed substance; And in thy book they were all written, Even the days that were ordained for me, When as yet there was none of them.

The phrases, "I was made in secret" and "curiously wrought in the lowest parts of the earth," refer to the psalmist's development in the womb (see Young, 1965, p. 76). Notice also that David employed the pronouns "me," "my," and "I" throughout the passage in reference to his own prenatal state. Such usage clearly shows that David was referring to himself, and one cannot talk about himself without having reference to a living human being. The Bible thus acknowledges that David was a human being while he inhabited his mother's womb (and prior to his birth).

Job, who was undergoing a terrible life crisis, cursed the day he was born when he said: "Why did I not **die from the womb**? Why did I not give up the ghost when my mother bore me?" (3:11). It is clear that if the fetus had **died** in the womb, prior to that it must have been **living**. Something (or someone) cannot die if it (or they) never lived. It also is of interest to observe that in Job 3:13-16, the patriarch listed several formerly-living-but-now-dead people with whom he would have had something in common **if** he had died *in utero*. Included in the list—along with kings and princes—was the child who experienced a "hidden untimely birth" (i.e., a miscarriage). Job considered the miscarried child to be in the same category as others who once lived but had died. Obviously, the Holy Spirit (Who guided the author of the book of Job in what he wrote) considered an unborn fetus as much a human being as a king, a prince, or a stillborn infant.

In the Old Testament, even the accidental termination of a pregnancy was a punishable crime. Consider Exodus 21:22—"If men strive together, and hurt a woman with child, so that her fruit depart, and yet no harm follows; he shall be surely fined, according as the woman's husband shall lay upon him...but if any harm follows, then thou shalt give life for life." The meaning of the passage is this: If the child was born prematurely as the result of this accident, but "no harm follows" (i.e. the child survived), then a fine was to be exacted; however, if "harm follows" (i.e., either mother or child died), then the guilty party was to be put to death. Look at it this way. Why would God exact such a severe punishment for the accidental **death** of an unborn child—if that child were not **living**?

The same understanding of the fetus as a living child is found within the pages of the New Testament. The angel Gabriel told Mary that "Elisabeth thy kinswoman, she also hath conceived **a son** in her old age" (Luke 1:36, emp. added). Please note that the conception resulted in neither an "it" nor a "thing," but in **a son**. In Luke 1:41,44, the Bible states (in speaking of Elisabeth, who was pregnant with John the Baptist) that "the babe leaped in her womb." The word for "babe" in these passages is the Greek term *brephos*, and is used here for an unborn fetus. The same word is used in both Luke 18:15 and Acts 7:19 for young or newborn children. It also is used in Luke 2:12,16 for the newborn Christ-child. *Brephos* therefore can refer to a young child, a newborn infant, or even an unborn fetus (see Thayer, 1958, p. 105). In each of these cases a living human being must be under consideration because the same word is used to describe all three.

The fact that the zygote/embryo/fetus is living (an inescapable conclusion supported by both weighty scientific and biblical evidence) thus becomes critically important in answering the question, "When does man receive his immortal nature?" When James observed that "the body apart from the spirit is dead" (2:26), the corollary automatically inherent in his statement became the fact that **if the body is living, then the spirit must be present**. Since at each stage of its development the zygote/embryo/fetus is living, it must have had a soul/spirit instilled at conception. No other view is in accord with both the biblical and scientific evidence.

3

THE NATURE OF THE SOUL

It is one thing to suggest that man possesses a soul or spirit. It is another to suggest that he receives such at conception. And it is still another to suggest that the soul/spirit survives the death of the physical body. [Since I previously documented the fact that on occasion within Scripture the words "soul" and "spirit" may be used synonymously, in order to avoid complicating the subject matter unnecessarily from this point on, I will employ them as such, rather than continuing to use the somewhat cumbersome "soul/spirit" designation.] As I mentioned in my introduction, there are a number of different views regarding the immortal nature of the soul.

Among those who accept the existence of the soul, there are some who are quite willing to believe that all men have such a spirit residing within them, but who are quite unwilling to believe that such is immortal, preferring to believe instead that this spiritual part is **purely temporal** (and thus lives only as long as our corporeal nature exists). Conversely, there are some who posit the idea that all humans not only possess an immortal soul, but that the souls of **all people** (regardless of their actions on Earth) will survive the death of the physical body in order to ultimately inhabit the heavenly realm with God. Others believe that while all men do indeed possess a soul,

only the soul of the faithful child of God has an immortal nature. That is to say, the souls of those who die outside of Christ are not immortal and perish when the body dies, while the soul of the Christian goes on into eternity. Still others believe that the souls of **both** the faithful child of God **and** the person outside of Christ are immortal—thereby surviving the death of the physical body in order to eventually inhabit either heaven (a place of eternal reward) or hell (a place of eternal punishment). Who is correct? What is the truth of the matter?

"TEMPORAL" SOULS?

Concerning the position that all men possess a soul, but that such is purely temporal and incapable of surviving the physical death of the body, Gilbert Thiele, a professor at Concordia Seminary in St. Louis, Missouri, wrote:

> We think it is consequently fair to say, to put it very bluntly, that when a man dies he is dead. The Bible when examined in its length and breadth knows of no disembodied condition in which man lives, temporarily, and certainly not permanently; it knows of neither a temporary nor a permanent human immortality as such (1958, p. 18).

Such a position, however, "to put it very bluntly," is indefensible in light of the multifarious teachings of Scripture. There are too many passages (e.g., Acts 7:59, Revelation 6:9, Matthew 10:28, et al.—discussed previously) which teach that the soul does, in fact, partake of an immortal nature. More will be said on this later in this book.

UNIVERSALISM

The idea that all humans possess an immortal soul, and that each and every one of those souls will survive the death of the physical body in order to inhabit the heavenly realm with God (regardless of their actions on Earth), is known as **universalism**. According to this view, all people will be saved; none will be lost. Advocates of this theory teach that since God is love (1 John 4:8), as well as a Sovereign

Who desires mercy rather than sacrifice (Matthew 9:13), then divine punishment must be viewed as merely remedial. God's loving, long-suffering nature, they suggest, cannot tolerate the loss of even one of His creatures since He is "not willing that any should perish" (2 Peter 3:9).

This view may be somewhat unusual, but it is by no means new. Origen, a well-known, third-century preacher (c. A.D. 185-254), was among the first to espouse it, and he has been joined by a parade of the famous (and not so famous) in the days since. The great poet, Alfred Lord Tennyson, in his poem, *In Memoriam*, advocated universalism. Scottish theologian and University of Glasgow divinity professor, William Barclay, was one of the concept's most ardent twentieth-century defenders. In his book, *The Plain Man Looks at the Apostles' Creed*, he wrote:

> It seems to us that if God is the God who is the God and Father of our Lord Jesus Christ, and if the total impression of the Gospel is true, we may dare to hope that when time ends God's family will be complete, for surely we must think in terms, not of a king who is satisfied with a victory which destroys his enemies, but of a Father who can never be content when even a single child of his is outside the circle of his love (1967, p. 239).

When you stop to think about it, it should not be at all surprising that such a view should receive widespread support. After all, it is a most comforting position. In his book, *How Can a God of Love Send People to Hell?*, British author John Benton addressed the inherent appeal of universalism when he wrote:

> I am sure that there is a part in all of us which would like to believe that that was true. If not, we are in danger of becoming very hard and unloving people indeed. We sympathize with the emotions which draw some people in the direction of universalism. But, in all honesty, it is impossible to interpret Jesus as teaching universalism (1985, p. 38).

I agree wholeheartedly with both parts of Benton's assessment. First, surely there is a twinge of desire in every human heart that would **like** to see everyone end up in heaven on the Day of Judgment. What an invigorating and refreshing belief—to entertain the hope that not a single human would lose his or her soul to the netherworld, but instead would walk the golden streets of heaven with God throughout all eternity. Second, however, in all honesty, it **is** impossible to interpret Jesus as teaching universalism. No amount of wishful thinking on our part can avoid the force of His arguments, or those of His inspired writers, on the subject of the final destination of those who live in rebellion to Heaven's will in the here and now.

Generally speaking, there are two distinct views regarding the mechanics of ultimate, universal salvation. First, there is the idea that entails the "remedial suffering" of which I spoke earlier. Prominent theologian Carl F.H. Henry referred to this notion when he wrote: "Hell itself is transformed from the ultimate state of the lost into a means of grace—a neo-Protestant purgatory of sorts" (1967, p. 27). Second, there is the idea known as "transcendentalism," which one writer expressed as follows:

> This idea held that every soul is a part of the "oversoul" of the universe. To use a common metaphor, man is a spark of the universal flame and will eventually return to it to be absorbed into the One Soul of all time.... Hell, according to this nebulous theory, is a training school for fragments of the Eternal Self which must be disciplined into final merger. The soul of man is only a spark of the divine flame and will finally be reabsorbed into it (Woodson, 1973, p. 60).

In both views, "hell" becomes simply a repository of the souls of people who need either: (a) a "second chance"—a fact brought to their attention by a little temporary "remedial suffering"; or (b) a brief period of disciplining/chastising to help them "shape up before they ship out" to the eternal joys of heaven. Such fanciful theories, of course, are not found within Scripture. Rather, they represent little more than wishful thinking on the part of those who, like universalists, hope to avoid the eternality of Hell that is associated in the Bible with God's divine mode, and term, of punishment. Anyone who suggests that repentance, reparation, and redemption are possible

after death (as both of these ideas plainly teach) simply does not understand the bulk of the Bible's teaching on such matters. The writer of the book of Hebrews wrote: "It is appointed unto men once to die, and after this cometh judgment" (9:27). The Lord Himself explained in Matthew 25:31-46 exactly what would happen to the wicked (whom He termed "goats," as opposed to the righteous, whom He labeled "sheep") on that great Judgment Day: "And these shall go away into **eternal punishment**, but the righteous into **eternal life**" (v. 46). Not much comfort for the universalist in these passages, is there?

In order to bolster their belief system, on occasion universalists have appealed to passages of Scripture that refer to God's concern for "all" men, or which show that the gift of life has been given to "all" people. Numerous statements from Paul, for example, have been quoted in potential support of universalism, including: (a) Romans 5:18 ("through one act of righteousness the free gift came unto **all** men to justification of life"); (b) Romans 11:25-26 ("**all** Israel shall be saved"); (c) 1 Corinthians 15:22 ("in Christ **all** shall be made alive"); and (d) 2 Corinthians 5:14 ("the love of Christ constraineth us; because we thus judge, that one died for **all**"). In his book, *Eternal Hope*, liberal theologian Emil Brunner wrote:

> That is the revealed will of God and the plan for the world which He discloses—a plan of **universal salvation**, of gathering all things into Christ. We hear not one word in the Bible of a dual plan, a plan of salvation and its polar opposite. The will of God has but one point, it is unambiguous and positive. It has one aim, not two (1954, p. 182, emp. added).

John A.T. Robinson, a bishop in the Church of England, wrote in a similar vein:

> In a universe of love there can be no heaven which tolerates a chamber of horrors, no hell for any which does not at the same time make it hell for God. He cannot endure that—for that would be the final mockery of His nature—and He will not (1949, p. 155).

Brunner and Robinson, however, are dead wrong. It is clear—when the passages from Paul's inspired pen are examined in their appropriate context—that they are not teaching the false concept of universalism. While the apostle taught that the Gospel of Christ is **universally available,** he did not teach that the Gospel would be **universally accepted!** In fact, he taught quite the opposite. In 2 Thessalonians 1:8, Paul referred to the fact that one day the Lord would return "from heaven with the angels of his power in flaming fire, rendering vengeance to them that know not God, and to them that **obey not the gospel** of our Lord Jesus." Interestingly, in the very next verse he wrote that such people "shall suffer punishment, **even eternal destruction from the face of the Lord** and from the glory of his might." Not much support here for universalism either, is there?

Universalism is an erroneous view that must be rejected, not only because it contradicts plain Bible teaching on the eternal fate of the wicked, but also because it makes a mockery of Christ's commission to His followers (whether in His day or in ours) as presented in Matthew 28:19-20. His command was: "Go ye therefore, and make disciples of all the nations, baptizing them into the name of the Father and of the Son and of the Holy Spirit: teaching them to observe all things whatsoever I commanded you." But, as Benton has pointed out:

> If everyone is saved, then Jesus' commission to his followers to preach the gospel and make disciples is pointless. People are going to be saved anyway. Universalism suffers from fatal defects. It is an alluring theory, but it does not fit the New Testament. Christianity is founded on the teachings of Christ and if we want to know what Christianity stands for, we must be prepared to face squarely what Jesus taught (1985, p. 38).

Indeed we must! But suggesting that all men everywhere will be saved—regardless of the lives they lead or the obedience to God's Word that they do or do not render—is tantamount to saying that Christ erred when He said that at His Second Coming He will "render unto every man **according to his deeds**" (Matthew 16:27, emp. added). If universalism is true, He likewise was mistaken when He taught that "every idle word that men shall speak, they shall give account thereof in the day of judgment. For by thy words thou shalt be justified, and by thy words **thou shalt be condemned**" (Matthew 12:36-37, emp. added). Similarly, Paul was wrong when he reminded first-century Christians: "So then each one of us shall give account of himself to God" (Romans 14:12).

True, universalism is an "alluring theory"—no doubt due in large part to the fact that it stresses only the goodness of God and none of His other equally important traits. Paul, however, "shrank not from declaring the **whole counsel** of God" (Acts 20:27, emp. added). Rather, he proclaimed: "Behold then the goodness and severity of God: toward them that fell, severity; but toward thee, God's goodness, if thou continue in his goodness: otherwise thou also shalt be cut off" (Romans 11:22). As David Brown observed:

> One of the great obligations of the church in getting lost men to see the error of their ways and obey the gospel is to preach the truth of the Bible regarding Hell and who is going there. To preach only the goodness of God is to omit part of the whole counsel of God (1999, p. 166).

And from the beginning of the Old Testament (e.g., Deuteronomy 4:2) to the end of the New (e.g., Revelation 22:18), the injunctions against altering, adding to, or deleting from God's Word are serious indeed. Universalism—as a doctrine that alters, adds to, and deletes from God's Word—should be (in fact, must be!) rejected.

ANNIHILATION FOR THE WICKED/ ETERNITY IN HEAVEN FOR THE RIGHTEOUS?

It hardly should surprise or shock us that atheists, agnostics, and infidels of every stripe have long rejected the notion (associated with the concept of an immortal soul) of an unending penalty for wickedness. First, they reject the idea of the existence of the soul itself and, second, they find the idea of eternal punishment utterly abhorrent.

As Brown noted: "One should not think it strange when men imagine doctrines that release them from the eternal consequences of a sinful life. What doctrine of the Bible has escaped corruption in the fertile imagination of rebellious men?" (1999, p. 161). Prominent British atheistic philosopher Antony Flew stated:

> I must confess that this subject of the doctrine of hell is one about which I find it very difficult to maintain my supposed national British calm and reserve. But let me, with what restraint I can muster, say that if anything can be known to be monstrously, inordinately wrong and unjust, it is the conduct of which this God is said to assume. If anything can be known to be just quite monstrously, inordinately, unquestionably unjust and evil, it is the conduct of a Being creating conscious creatures, whether human or animal, in the full knowledge, and with the intention, that these creatures should be maintained by His sustaining power eternally in infinite and unlimited torment. I speak of this with what little restraint I can muster because, if anything seems clear to me about good and evil, just and unjust, it is clear to me that this is monstrous (1977, pp. 84-85).

The famous nineteenth-century American agnostic, Robert G. Ingersoll (1833-1899), wrote:

> This idea of hell was born of ignorance, brutality, fear, cowardice, and revenge. This idea testifies that our remote ancestors were the lowest beasts. Only from the dens, lairs, and caves, only from the mouths filled with cruel fangs, only from hearts of fear and hatred, only from the conscience of hunger and lust, only from the lowest and most debased could come this cruel, heartless, and bestial of all dogmas... (as quoted in Lewis, 1983, p. 90).

Ingersoll then went on to say:

> The idea of hell is born of revenge and brutality. I have no respect for any human being who believes in it. I have no respect for any man who preaches it. I dislike this doctrine. I hate it, despise, and defy it. The doctrine of hell is infamous beyond words (as quoted in Stacey, 1977, p. 59).

In his widely circulated essay, *Why I Am Not a Christian*, English agnostic philosopher Bertrand Russell commented: "I must say that I think all this doctrine, that hell-fire is a punishment for sin, is a doctrine of cruelty. It is a doctrine that put cruelty into the world and gave the world generations of cruel torture..." (1967, p. 18).

But what about those who believe in God and who accept as genuine the existence of the soul? Some among that number believe that while all men do indeed possess a soul, **only that of the faithful child of God has an immortal nature**. That is to say, the souls of those who die outside of Christ are not immortal and thus perish when the body dies, while the soul of the Christian goes into eternity (i.e., heaven). Others believe that the souls of **both** the faithful child of God **and** the person outside of Christ are immortal—thereby surviving the death of the physical body in order to eventually inhabit either a place of eternal reward (heaven) or a place of eternal punishment (hell). Which position is correct?

To be sure, there have been those who have taught that **only** the souls of the faithful are immortal, while those of the unfaithful perish at their physical death (a concept known as annihilationism). And again, this is not a new doctrine. In the July 1852 issue of *Christian Magazine*, a popular preacher from Nashville, Tennessee, Jesse B. Ferguson, asked:

> Is Hell a dungeon dug by Almighty hands before man was born, into which the wicked are to be plunged? And is the salvation upon the preacher's lips a salvation from such a Hell? For ourself, we rejoice to say it, we never believed, and upon the evidence so far offered, never can believe it (1852, p. 202).

In an article titled "Fire, Then Nothing" written in *Christianity Today* 135 years later, denominational scholar Clark Pinnock suggested that the souls of the wicked are annihilated at physical death (1987). In his book, *The Fire That Consumes*, Edward W. Fudge taught the same concept when he wrote: "The wicked, following whatever degree and duration of pain that God may justly inflict, will finally and truly die, perish and **become extinct for ever and ever**" (1982, p. 425, emp. added). Interestingly, Fudge's book drew rave reviews from certain quarters.

John N. Clayton, a self-proclaimed former-atheist-turned-Christian who lectures frequently on Christian evidences, and who is known chiefly for his numerous compromises of the Genesis account of creation, edits a small, bi-monthly journal titled *Does God Exist?* In the September/October 1990 issue, he reviewed *The Fire That Consumes* and said:

> One of the most frequent challenges of atheists during our lectures is the question of the reasonableness of the concept of hell. Why would a loving, caring, merciful God create man as he is, **knowing** that man would sin, reject God, and be condemned to eternal punishment? I have had to plead ignorance in this area because I had no logical answer that was consistent with the Bible.... I have never been able to be comfortable with the position that a person who rejected God should suffer forever and ever and ever (1990a, p. 20, emp. in orig.).

Clayton first described Fudge's book as "an exhaustive, scholarly study of the subject of hell," then confidently affirmed that it "will open many new viewpoints to any thinking reader," and finally concluded by saying: "**I recommend this book highly** to the serious student of the Bible who is not afraid to have some traditions challenged" (pp. 20-21, emp. added). Strangely, in the 1990 edition of his book, *The Source*, Clayton recommended Fudge's volume as one that contained "reasonably accurate **scientific** material"—even though the book deals solely with **theological** matters (1990b, pp. 190-191). At his weekend seminars on Christian evidences, Mr. Clayton routinely makes available a handout in which he recommends certain books that he believes would be of benefit to each of the seminar participants. Fudge's book is included on that handout. And, in the 1991 edition of the *Teacher's Guide* that accompanies his *Does God Exist? Christian Evidences Intermediate Course*, Clayton offered the following suggestion in regard to lesson number six:

One approach that is very useful, although somewhat controversial, is Edward Fudge's book *The Fire That Consumes*. Fudge deals with the subject of this lesson and takes the position that hell is the destruction of the soul (1991, p. 25, emp. added).

In April 1988, while speaking on the subject of "A Christian Response to the New Age Movement" at the annual Pepperdine University lectures in Malibu, California, best-selling author F. LaGard Smith asked the members of his audience:

> I also wonder if you feel as uncomfortable as I do in our traditional view of hell. Do you readily accept the traditional view of hell that says God sort of dangles you over the fires that burn day and night?... Is that what hell is all about? Haven't you struggled with the idea of how there can be a loving God and anywhere in his presence permit that to exist? Doesn't it seem like cruel and unusual punishment? (1988).

In that same lecture, Smith strenuously argued that God will "destroy it [the soul—BT]. Not punish it. Not dangle it. Not torture it. **Destroy it**!" (1988). Three years later, in October 1991, Wayne Jackson (as editor of the *Christian Courier*) wrote LaGard Smith to ask him about his position on the destiny of the souls of the wicked. Within a week, Smith replied via a five-page, handwritten letter in which he admitted that he believed in "the possibility that part of the ultimate punishment of the wicked is total destruction of their souls" (as quoted in Jackson, 1993, p. 65; see Jackson, 1998, 33[9]: 35 for a discussion of, and response to, Smith's subsequent claim that he has been "misunderstood" in regard to his views on the annihilation of the soul).

Another advocate of the view that the souls of the wicked will be annihilated is Alan Pickering who, in the 1980s, presented seminars around the country under the title of "Sharpening the Sword." In December of 1986, he spoke at the Central Church of Christ in Stockton, California and advocated the view that the souls of the wicked, after a limited period of punishment, will cease to exist. As he had done with LaGard Smith, Wayne Jackson (who resides in

Stockton) wrote Pickering to inquire if the material available on audio tape from his lectures did, in fact, accurately represent his views. In a subsequent telephone conversation a few days later, Mr. Pickering acknowledged that it did, and even went so far as to state that the concept of eternal conscious punishment for the wicked was a "slap in the face of God." He then challenged Wayne to a public debate on the matter—a challenge he later retracted when his offer was accepted (see Jackson, 1987, 23[8]:31).

In addition to those mentioned above, well-known creationist Robert L. Whitelaw defended the annihilationist position in his work, *Can There be Eternal Life Apart from Christ?*, when he wrote of those who die outside of Christ:

> Yet nowhere among all the pillars of theological orthodoxy ...do we find a work of solid exegesis proving the notion of man's innate immortality to be the teaching of the Bible, based on the whole counsel of Scripture.... Search Scripture as you will, there is no hint of any other kind of life or existence beyond Judgment Day for any being, human or demonic.... We have shown that nowhere in Scripture does God describe the state of lost mankind after Judgment Day as "life," "living," or even unconscious existence (1991, pp. 2,11).

The list of prominent religionists who have supported, and continue to support, the annihilationist position could be extended with ease. What, then, should be our response to this curious dogma?

At the outset, we should acknowledge clear biblical instruction that the soul of the faithful child of God will enjoy eternity forever in heaven. Such a concept is established beyond doubt in both the Old and New Testaments. As early as the book of Genesis, we read that Abraham "was gathered to his people" (25:8). Obviously, this cannot mean that Abraham was buried with his ancestors since "his people" were buried in Ur of the Chaldees and in Haran. Abraham, on the other hand, was buried in the cave of Machpelah (25:9). The same words were used of Aaron (Numbers 20:24,26) and Moses (Numbers 27:13; 31:2; Deuteronomy 32:50). Certainly, in their individual cases this cannot possibly have reference to their interment in some sort of family tomb or burial plot. Gesenius, in his *Hebrew-Chaldee Lexicon to the Old Testament,* noted that "this being gathered to one's people, or fathers, is expressly distinguished both from death and from burial" (1979, p. 67).

When David's son (born as a result of his adultery with Bathsheba) died shortly after birth, the shattered sovereign said:

> While the child was yet alive, I fasted and wept: for I said, "Who knoweth whether Jehovah will not be gracious to me, that the child may live?" But now he is dead, wherefore should I fast? Can I bring him back again? **I shall go to him**, but he will not return to me (2 Samuel 12:22-23, emp. added).

Amidst his much suffering, the patriarch Job said:

> But as for me I know that my Redeemer liveth, and at last he will stand upon the earth: And after my skin, even this body, is destroyed, **then without my flesh shall I see God**; Whom I, even I, shall see, on my side, and mine eyes shall behold, and not as a stranger (Job 19:25-27, emp. added).

When Elijah raised the widow's son from the dead (1 Kings 17:21-22), Scripture states:

> And he stretched himself upon the child three times, and cried unto Jehovah, and said, "O Jehovah my God, I pray thee, let this child's soul come into him again." And Jehovah hearkened unto the voice of Elijah; and the soul of the child came into him again, and he revived.

Because of the fact that we have access to later revelation, such as that contained in James 2:26 which states that "the body apart from the spirit is dead," we understand that in 1 Kings 17 the word soul (*nephesh*) is employed to speak of the immortal nature of the young man (i.e., his soul/spirit). His body was dead due to the fact that his spirit had departed. Elijah prayed that it be returned, and it was— a fact that certainly precludes its annihilation. In His discussion with Martha concerning life after death, Jesus said: "I am the resurrection, and the life: he that believeth on me, though he die, yet shall he live; and **whosoever liveth and believeth on me shall never die**" (John 11:25-27, emp. added; cf. Revelation 6:9).

On one occasion while Saul was serving as king of Israel, the Philistines were amassing for war, "and when Saul saw the host of the Philistines, he was afraid, and his heart trembled greatly. And when Saul inquired of Jehovah, Jehovah answered him not" (1 Samuel 28:5). Saul, therefore—in violation of both God's law (Deuteronomy 18:10) and Israelite law (1 Samuel 28:9)—sought out a "medium" whom he hoped could "conjure up" Samuel's long-departed spirit (1 Samuel 28:3 records that "Samuel was dead, and all Israel had lamented him, and buried him in Ramah"), from whom he intended to seek counsel and comfort. The medium (known as "the witch of Endor") somehow contacted Samuel and quickly expressed her great fear at the sight of his disembodied spirit (1 Samuel 28:12). Samuel's response documents the fact that he did not relish a call back to this world: "Why hast thou disquieted me, to bring me up?" (28:15). If his immortal nature had been annihilated at his death, how, then, was he able to return (and even to complain about having to do so!)? Remember also that the spirits of Moses and Elijah not only joined Christ on a mountaintop in Palestine, but spoke to Him as well (Luke 9:30-31). If those spirits had ceased to exist at their owners' demise, how could they have done either?

That death is **not** total annihilation is clear from the words of Christ in John 5:28-29: "The hour cometh in which **all** that are in the tombs shall hear his voice, and **shall come forth**." In Luke 8:55, the account is recorded of Christ raising Jairus' daughter from the dead. The text reads as follows: "And her spirit (*pneuma*) returned, and she rose up immediately." If her spirit had been annihilated, it hardly could have "returned." And, at the risk of repeating myself, I would like to point out that Christ's discussion with the Sadducees (as recorded in Matthew 22) must not be overlooked in this context. On that occasion, the Lord quoted from Exodus 3:6 where God had said to Moses: "I am the God of Abraham, and the God of Isaac, and the God of Jacob." Yet as Christ went on to state (and as the Sadducees accepted as true), "God is not the God of the dead, but of the living" (22:32). Abraham, Isaac, and Jacob had been dead and in their graves for many years. Since we know from Christ's own words (and the inability of the Sadducees to offer any rebuttal whatsoever) that "God is not the God of the dead, but of the living," the point is obvious. Abraham, Isaac, and Jacob still must have been living. How so? The answer, of course, lies in the fact that while their bodies had died, their souls had not. And since their immortal nature lived on, it could not have been annihilated at their physical demise.

On one occasion during Jesus' earthly ministry, He discussed the importance of the soul with His disciples when He said: "For what shall it profit a man, if he shall gain the whole world, and lose his own soul? Or what shall a man give in exchange for his soul?" (Mark 8: 36-37). Indeed, if the immortal nature of man is annihilated at the death of the body, what was Christ's point? Would not a man benefit by exchanging "annihilation" for the "whole world"?

What did Christ mean, then, when He warned: "Be not afraid of them that kill the body, but are not able to kill the soul: but rather fear him who is able to destroy both soul and body in hell" (Matthew 10: 28)? As D.M. Lake observed, at the very least this "does imply a transcendental reality that is in some cases independent of the body. This seems to be the force of Jesus' statement [in] Matthew 10:28" (1976, 5:497). The "destruction" of which Jesus spoke was described by the apostle John as the "second death."

> The devil that deceived them was cast into the lake of fire and brimstone, where are also the beast and the false prophet; and they shall be tormented day and night **for ever and ever**.... And they were judged every man according to their works. And death and Hades were cast into the lake of fire. This is the second death, even the lake of fire (Revelation 20:10-14, emp. added).

The eternal nature of that second death is evident from John's description of the wicked men who "shall drink of the wine of the wrath of God...and shall be tormented with fire and brimstone...and **the smoke of their torment goeth up for ever and ever; and they have no rest day and night**" (Revelation 14:10-11, emp. added).

Furthermore, the position that **only** the souls of the faithful are immortal, while those of "lost mankind" are annihilated at their physical death, is both terribly wrong and squarely at odds with the teachings of God's Word. The Scriptures plainly indicate that the disobedient are to be subjected to eternal punishment. In Matthew 25:46, Jesus said that the wicked would "go away into **eternal** punishment, but the righteous into eternal life." In his second epistle to the Christians at Thessalonica, Paul wrote specifically of "them that know not God" and "obey not the gospel of our Lord Jesus Christ" as those "who shall suffer punishment, even **eternal** destruction from the face of the Lord and from the glory of his might" (1:8-9). In addressing this point, Wayne Jackson wrote:

> There is, however, no punishment, or suffering, apart of consciousness. And yet, consciousness (knowledge, awareness) is a characteristic of the spirit (1 Cor. 2:11). One must necessarily infer, therefore, that the spirit (our soul) of man will exist in an eternal conscious state. Jesus once said regarding the traitor Judas that it would have been better for that man had he never been born (Mark 14:21). If Judas did not exist before his earthly life, and yet was to be annihilated eventually, how does the Lord's statement make sense? How is non-existence better than non-existence? (1991, 27[5]:19).

Additionally, the New Testament account (recorded in Luke 16) that describes Christ's discussion of two men who died under different circumstances merits serious consideration here. One, Lazarus, went to Abraham's bosom (a synonym for paradise). The other, an unnamed rich man, found himself in the portion of hades where, he exclaimed, "I am tormented in this flame" (16:22-24). Thus, the spirits of the two men, upon leaving their bodies, were alive, conscious, and even able to converse —although they were in two significantly different places. One was "comforted," one was "tormented," and a great gulf separated them (Luke 16:26). When the rich man requested that Lazarus be allowed to return to Earth to warn his five siblings not to follow him to such a terrible place, Abraham denied his request and responded: "If they hear not Moses and the prophets, neither will they be persuaded **if one rise from the dead**" (16: 31). The key phrase here, of course, is "**if** one rise from the dead." Abraham did not say that such was **impossible**; rather, he indicated that it was **inappropriate**. There is a vast difference in the two. Lazarus **could** have returned, but was not allowed to do so. The simple fact of the matter is that Abraham's spirit, Lazarus' spirit, and the rich man's spirit all continued to exist beyond the grave. That the rich man found himself in a place (and state) of torment demolishes the idea that the souls of the wicked do not survive this life. That the souls of the wicked endure torment "for ever and ever, and have no rest day and night" (Revelation 14:10-11) demolishes the idea that the souls of the wicked are annihilated at any point following the death of the physical body.

Some, of course, have lamented that since the account in Luke 16 is "only" a parable, neither its message nor its implications may be taken literally. Such a notion, however, overlooks several important points regarding the nature of the text itself. First, notice that Christ referred to two of the three people **by name**. He mentioned both Abraham and Lazarus. As Tim Rice has observed:

> Those of the "parable" philosophy who disparage of an eternal hell's existence think that the rich man was a fictional character. They even ignore the fact that Lazarus' name is the **only proper name ever used in a parable** (if this be a parable). The key to the question of whether this account is strictly imagery is not just the consideration of the rich man or Lazarus, but Abraham! In Matthew 22:32, Jesus Himself claimed that Abraham continued to live in the spiritual realm. The narrative of the rich man and Lazarus places Lazarus in the presence of a literal Old Testament figure, Abraham, who was existing in some realm at that time (1987, 15[1]:6, parenthetical comment in orig., emp. added).

Second, what, exactly, was Christ's point in relating this account? Was He attempting to deceive his hearers? Was He merely trying to "scare" them into submission to Heaven's will? Rice has inquired:

If the covetous do not really enter a realm where they can think, remember, and where they desire relief and are bound from salvation by a great gulf, why would Jesus con his hearers by discussing such a realm? The thrust of his narrative was to make his hearers avoid the position in which the rich man found himself, i.e., torment (15[1]:6).

Third, compare the condition of the rich man (as depicted by Jesus) with a similar passage also from the lips of the Lord. That covetous fellow described his horrible fate when he remarked: "I am tormented in this **flame**" (Luke 16:24, emp. added). In Matthew 25: 41, the Lord said to those who were doomed: "Depart from me, ye cursed, into the eternal **fire** which is prepared for the devil and his angels." Acknowledging what Christ taught in Matthew 25, upon what basis could we draw the conclusion that He was teaching anything different in Luke 16? Was He not attempting to warn His hearers in both instances of a **literal** place where they **(literally!)** did not want to go?

Fourth, Jesus was not in the habit of using the "abstract" in His parables. Rather, He used substantive examples of events that were based on the everyday lives of His audience. When He presented for His audience's consideration the parables of the sower (Matthew 13: 3-23), the tares (Matthew 13:24-30), or the lost coin (Luke 15:8-10), He was speaking about things that literally could have happened. Similarly, the things He discussed in the account of the rich man and Lazarus could have happened, since additional passages (e.g., Matthew 25, Jude 7, et al.) confirm the existence of a spirit realm such as the one described by the Lord in Luke 16. As Rice has noted: "Even if this account **were** a parable, the realm described is real" (15[1]:6, emp. in orig.). David Brown reasoned in a comparable fashion.

> If, for the sake of argument, we admit that Luke 16:19-31 is a parable, annihilationists can get no solace from such an admission. Why is this the case? It is because all parables teach the truth. Now, what is the truth taught in the case of the "Rich

man and Lazarus"? At death wicked men go into torment, and saved men into a place of comfort and rest. However, we do not admit that the passage is a parable. It bears no marks of a parable. Quite the contrary when the passage is analyzed. Please note that Jesus emphatically declared in no uncertain terms, "There was a certain rich man...." Question: Was there? Jesus answers, "There was...." Our Lord declared in no uncertain terms, "...there was a certain beggar named Lazarus...." Question: Was there? Jesus answers, "There was...." These two men lived on earth, died, and according to their conduct on earth, went to their respective places in the hadean world to await the end of the world, the resurrection, and the Judgment. Our Lord selected them to teach us a lesson regarding what transpired at death for the wicked and the blest (1999, pp. 170-171, emp. in orig.).

In a similar vein, Daniel Denham remarked:

The absurdity of the argument is also seen in that as a "parable," it would **still** teach the same thing: for a parable by definition draws the force of its imagery from the reality of the action or thing with which the similitude is made. It is the fact of and reality of sowing crops, for instance, that provides the substance for the Lord's lesson in the Parable of the Sower, and it was the common rites of matrimony upon which the Lord drew for emphasis and color in the Parable of the Wise and Foolish Virgins. To use the account of Luke 16:19ff. as a parable (granting for the moment it is such) would not be possible, except that first such a condition of things ascribed therein to Hades did, in fact, exist!

Another thing about parables is that the truth displayed by the story is always greater in degree and importance than the story itself due to the consequences entailed. Planting seeds indeed was necessary for one to have crops to harvest, but how much more important is the planting of the Word of God? It is far worse not to be ready when the Master comes, than to be one of the foolish maids who are left knocking at the barred door of an earthly wedding! It would be far worse to be in the spiritual plight of the Pharisees than to be the Rich Man in Hades (1998, p. 621, emp. and parenthetical comment in orig.).

Furthermore, there are several other important points that practically leap off the pages of Scripture, and that need to be examined in this particular context. First, those who argue for the ultimate annihilation of the souls of the wicked apparently have failed to comprehend both the abominable, repulsive nature of man's sin against God and the inestimable, unspeakable price Heaven paid to redeem rebellious man from its clutches. Second, they appear not to have grasped the necessity or purpose of punishment in God's grand plan. Third, they evidently have overlooked (or ignored) the straightforward teaching of the Scriptures on the eternal fate of the wicked. And fourth, they seem to have missed the telling fact that every single argument made against the existence of an eternal Hell likewise can be leveled against the existence of an eternal heaven. Each of these deserves close scrutiny.

4

MAN'S SOUL AND MAN'S SIN

Of all the living beings that dwell on planet Earth, one solitary creature was made "in the image of God" (Genesis 1:26-27). Mankind was not created in the physical image of God, of course, because God, as a Spirit Being, has no physical image (John 4:24; Luke 24:39; Matthew 16:17). Rather, mankind was fashioned in the spiritual, rational, emotional, and volitional image of God (Ephesians 4:24; John 5:39-40; 7:17; Joshua 24:15; Isaiah 7:15). Humans are superior to all other creatures on Earth. No other living being has been given the faculties, capacities, potential, capabilities, or worth that God instilled in each man and woman. Indeed, humankind is the peak, the pinnacle, the apex of God's creation. In its lofty position as the zenith of God's creative genius, mankind was endowed with certain responsibilities. Men and women were to be the stewards of the entire Earth (Genesis 1:28). They were to glorify God in their daily existence (Isaiah 43:7). And, they were to consider it their "whole duty" to serve the Creator faithfully throughout their brief sojourn on this planet (Ecclesiastes 12:13).

Unfortunately, however, as the first man and woman, Adam and Eve used their volitional powers—and the free moral agency based on those powers—to rebel against their Maker. Finite man made some horribly evil choices, and thereafter found himself in the spiritual state designated biblically as "sin." The Old Testament not only pictures in vivid fashion the entrance of sin into the world through Adam and Eve (Genesis 3), but also alludes to the ubiquity of sin throughout the human race when it says: "There is no man that sinneth not" (1 Kings 8:46). Throughout its thirty-nine books, the Old Covenant discusses over and over sin's presence amidst humanity, as well as its destructive consequences. The great prophet Isaiah reminded God's people:

> Behold, Jehovah's hand is not shortened that it cannot save; neither his ear heavy that it cannot hear: but your iniquities have separated between you and your God, and your sins have hid his face from you, so that he will not hear (Isaiah 59:1-2).

The New Testament is no less clear in its assessment. The apostle John wrote: "Every one that doeth sin doeth also lawlessness; and sin is lawlessness" (1 John 3:4). Thus, sin is defined as the act of transgressing God's law. In fact, Paul observed that "where there is no law, neither is there transgression" (Romans 4:15). Had there been no law, there would have been no sin. But God **had** instituted divine law. And mankind freely chose to transgress that law. Paul reaffirmed the Old Testament concept of the universality of sin when he stated that "all have sinned, and fall short of the glory of God" (Romans 3:23).

As a result, mankind's predicament became serious indeed. Ezekiel lamented: "The soul that sinneth, it shall die" (18:20a). Once again, the New Testament writers reaffirmed such a concept. Paul wrote: "Therefore, as through one man sin entered into the world, and death through sin; and so death passed unto all men, for that all sinned" (Romans 5:12). He then added that "the wages of sin is death" (Romans 6:23). Years later, James would write: "But each man is tempted, when he is drawn away by his own lust, and enticed. Then the lust, when it hath conceived, beareth sin: and the sin, when it is full-grown, bringeth forth death" (James 1:15-16). As a result of mankind's sin, God placed the curse of death on the human race. While all men and women must die **physically** as a result of Adam and Eve's sin, each person dies **spiritually** for his or her own sins. Each person is responsible for himself, spiritually speaking. The theological position which states that we inherit the guilt of Adam's sin is utterly false. We do not inherit the **guilt**; we inherit the **consequences**. In Ezekiel 18:20, the prophet went on to say:

> The son shall not bear the iniquity of the father, neither shall the father bear the iniquity of the son: the righteousness of the righteous shall be upon him, and the wickedness of the wicked shall be upon him.

The reality of sin is all around us, and its effects permeate every aspect of our lives. Disease and death were introduced into this world as a direct consequence of man's sin (Genesis 2:17; Romans 5:12). Many features of the Earth's surface that allow for such tragedies as earthquakes, tornadoes, hurricanes, violent thunderstorms, etc., can be traced directly to the Great Flood of Noah's day (which came as the result of man's sin; Genesis 6:5ff.). The communication problems that man experiences, due to the multiplicity of human languages, are traceable to ambitious rebellion on the part of our ancestors (Genesis 11:1-9). Man generally is without the peace of mind for which his heart longs (just consider the number of psychiatrists in the Yellow Pages!). Isaiah opined: "They have made them crooked paths; whosoever goeth therein doth not know peace" (59:8; cf. 57:21). By sinning, man created a yawning chasm between himself and God (Isaiah 59:2). In his book, *Created in God's Image*, Anthony Hoekema addressed this chasm when he wrote:

> Sin is always related to God and his will. Many people consider what Christians call **sin** mere imperfection—the kind of imperfection that is a normal aspect of human nature. "Nobody's perfect," "everybody makes mistakes," "you're only human," and similar statements express this kind of thinking. Over against this we must insist that, according to Scripture, sin is always a transgression of the law of God.... Sin is

therefore fundamentally opposition to God, rebellion against God, which roots in hatred to God.... [T]hough fallen man still bears the image of God, he now functions wrongly as an image-bearer of God. This, in fact, makes sin all the more heinous. Sin is a perverse way of using God-given and God-reflecting powers (1986, pp. 169,171, emp. in orig.).

The well-known British writer, C.S. Lewis, expressed this very fact in a most unforgettable manner via a personal letter to one of his friends when he wrote:

[I]ndeed the only way in which I can make real to myself what theology teaches about the heinousness of sin is to remember that every sin is the distortion of an energy breathed into us.... We poison the wine as He decants it into us; murder a melody He would play with us as the instrument. We caricature the self-portrait He would paint. Hence all sin, whatever else it is, is sacrilege (1966, pp. 71-72).

Unless remedied, this rebellion, this sacrilege, will result in man's being unable to escape what the Son of God Himself called the "judgment of hell" (Matthew 23:33)—the end result of which is eternal separation from God throughout all eternity (Revelation 21:8; 22:18-19).

The key phrase in the above discussion, of course, is **unless remedied**. The question then becomes: Has Heaven provided such a remedy? Thankfully, the answer is "yes." One thing is certain, however. God had no **obligation** to provide a means of salvation for the ungrateful creature that so haughtily turned away from Him, His law, and His beneficence. The Scriptures make this apparent when they discuss the fact that angels sinned (2 Peter 2:4; Jude 6), and yet "not to angels doth he give help, but he giveth help to the seed of Abraham" (Hebrews 2:16). The rebellious creatures that once inhabited the heavenly portals were not provided a redemptive plan. But man was! Little wonder, then, that the psalmist was moved to ask: "What is **man**, that thou art mindful of **him**?" (8:4, emp. added).

Why would God go to such great lengths for mankind, when His mercy was not even extended to the angels that once surrounded His throne? Whatever answers may be proffered, there can be little doubt that the Creator's efforts on behalf of sinful man are the direct result of pure, unadulterated love. As a God of love (1 John 4:8), He acted out of a genuine concern, not for His own desires, but rather for those of His creation. And let us be forthright in acknowledging that Jehovah's love for mankind was completely **undeserved**. The Scriptures make it clear that God decided to offer salvation—our "way home" —even though we were ungodly, sinners, and enemies (note the specific use of those terms in Romans 5:6-10). The apostle John rejoiced in the fact that: "Herein is love, not that we loved God, but that He loved us" (1 John 4:10). God's love is universal, and thus not discriminatory in any fashion (John 3:16). He would have **all men** to be saved (1 Timothy 2:4)—**if they would be** (John 5:40)—for He is not willing that **any** should perish (2 Peter 3:9). And, further, Deity's love is unquenchable (read Romans 8:35-39 and be thrilled!). Only man's wanton rejection of God's love can put him beyond the practical appropriation of Heaven's offer of mercy and grace.

Did God understand that man would rebel, and stand in eventual need of salvation from the perilous state of his own sinful condition? The Scriptures make it clear that He did. Inspiration speaks of a divine plan set in place even "before the foundation of the world" (Ephesians 1:4; 1 Peter 1:20). After the initial fall of man, humankind dredged itself deeper and deeper into wickedness. When approximately a century of preaching by the righteous Noah failed to bring mankind back to God, Jehovah sent a global flood to purge the Earth (Genesis 6-8). From the faithful Noah, several generations later, the renowned Abraham descended, and, through him, the Hebrew nation. From that nation, the Messiah—God-incarnate—one day would come.

Some four centuries following Abraham, the Lord, through His servant Moses, gave to the Hebrews the written revelation that came to be known as the Law of Moses. Basically, this law-system had three purposes. First, its intent was to define sin and sharpen Israel's awareness of it. To use Paul's expression in the New Testament, the Law made "sin exceeding sinful" (Romans 7:7,13). Second, the law was designed to show man that he could not save himself via his own effort, or as a result of his own merit. The Law demanded perfect obedience, and since no mere man could keep it perfectly, each stood condemned (Galatians 3:10-11). Thus, the Law underscored the need for a **Savior**—Someone Who could do for us what we were unable to do for ourselves. Third, in harmony with that need, the Old Testament pointed the way toward the coming of the Messiah. He was to be Immanuel—"God with us" (Matthew 1:23). Jehovah left no stone unturned in preparing the world for the coming of the One Who was to save mankind.

One of God's attributes, as expressed within Scripture, is that He is an absolutely **holy** Being (cf. Isaiah 6:3 and Revelation 4:8). As such, He simply cannot ignore the fact of sin. The prophet Habakkuk wrote: "Your eyes are too pure to look on evil; you cannot tolerate wrong" (1:13). Yet, another of God's attributes is that He is absolutely **just**. Righteousness and justice are the very foundation of His throne (Psalm 89:14). The irresistible truth arising from the fact that God is both holy and just is **that sin must be punished!** If God were a cold, vengeful Creator (as some infidels wrongly assert), He simply could have banished mankind from His divine presence forever, and that would have been the end of the matter. But the truth is, He is not that kind of God! Our Creator is loving (1 John 4:8), and "rich in mercy" (Ephesians 2:4). When justice is meted out, we **receive what we deserve**. When mercy is extended, we **do not receive what we deserve**. When grace is bestowed, we **receive what we do not deserve**.

Thus, the problem became: How could a loving, merciful God pardon a wickedly rebellious humanity? Paul addressed this very matter in Romans 3. How could God be just, and yet a justifier of sinful man? The answer: He would find someone to stand in for us—someone to receive **His** retribution, and to bear **our** punishment.

That "someone" would be Jesus Christ, the Son of God. He would become a substitutionary sacrifice, and personally would pay the price for human salvation. Paul wrote: "Him who knew no sin he made to be sin on our behalf that we might become the righteousness of God in him" (2 Corinthians 5:21). In one of the most moving tributes ever written to the Son of God, Isaiah summarized the situation as follows:

> Surely he hath borne our griefs, and carried our sorrows; yet we did esteem him stricken, smitten of God, and afflicted. But he was wounded for our transgressions, he was bruised for our iniquities; the chastisement of our peace was upon him; and with his stripes we are healed. All we like sheep have gone astray; we have turned everyone to his own way; and Jehovah hath laid on him the iniquity of us all.... He bare the sin of many, and made intercession for the transgressors (53:4-6, 12).

Paul reminded the first-century Christians in Rome:

> Scarcely for a righteous man will one die: for peradventure for the good man some one would even dare to die. But God commendeth his own love toward us, in that, while we were yet sinners, Christ died for us (Romans 5:7-8).

Jehovah's intent was to extend grace and mercy freely—on the basis of the redemptive life and death of His Son (Romans 3:24ff.). Though part of the Godhead, Christ took upon Himself the form of a man. He came to Earth as a human being (John 1:1-4,14; Philippians 2:5-11; 1 Timothy 3:16), and thus shared our full nature and life-experience. He even was tempted in all points exactly as we are, yet He never yielded to that temptation and sinned (Hebrew 4:15).

There was no happy solution to the justice/mercy dilemma. There was no way by which God could remain just (justice demands that the wages of sin be paid), and yet save His Son from death. Christ was abandoned to the cross so that mercy could be extended to sinners who stood condemned (Galatians 3:10). God could not save sinners by fiat—upon the ground of mere authority alone—without violating His own attribute of divine justice. Paul discussed God's response to this problem in Romans 3:24-26:

Being justified freely by his grace through the redemption that is in Christ Jesus; whom God set forth to be a propitiation, through faith, in his blood...for the showing of his righteousness...that he might himself be just and the justifier of him that hath faith in Jesus.

Man's salvation was no arbitrary arrangement. God did not decide merely to consider man a sinner, and then determine to save him upon a principle of mercy. Sin placed man in a state of antagonism toward God. Sinners are condemned because they have violated God's law, and because God's justice cannot permit Him to ignore sin. Sin could be forgiven only as a result of the vicarious death of God's Son. Because sinners are redeemed by the sacrifice of Christ, and not because of their own righteousness, they are sanctified by the mercy and grace of God. Our sins were borne by Jesus on the cross. Since Christ was tested, tempted, and tried (Isaiah 28:16), and yet found perfect (2 Corinthians 5:21; 1 Peter 2:22), He alone could satisfy Heaven's requirement for justice. He alone could serve as the "propitiation" (i.e., an atoning sacrifice) for our sins. Just as the lamb without blemish that was used in Old Testament sacrifices could be the (temporary) propitiation for the Israelites' sins, so the "Lamb of God" (John 1:29) could be the (permanent) propitiation for mankind's sins.

In the death of the Lamb of God, divine justice was satisfied; in the gift of Christ, Heaven's mercy and grace were extended. When humans became the recipients of heaven's grace, the unfathomable happened. God—our Justifiable Accuser—became our Vindicator. He extended to us His wonderful love, as expressed by His mercy and grace. He paid our debt so that we, like undeserving Barabbas (Matthew 27:26), might be set free. In this fashion, God could be just and, at the same time, Justifier of all who believe in and obey His Son. By refusing to extend mercy to Jesus as He hung on the cross, God was able to extend mercy to mankind—**if** mankind was willing to submit in obedience to His commands.

THE NECESSITY AND
PURPOSE OF PUNISHMENT

But what if God does not exist? Or what if He does, but mankind **is unwilling to submit to Him**? What then? First, of course, if there is no Creator, if everything ultimately springs from natural causes and this life is all there is, what would it matter **how** man acts? If he is merely the last in a long chain of evolutionary accidents, why should his conduct be of any concern at all? The late, eminent evolutionist of Harvard University, George Gaylord Simpson, considered this point and concluded:

> Discovery that the universe apart from man or before his coming lacks and lacked any purpose or plan has the inevitable corollary that the workings of the universe cannot provide any automatic, universal, eternal, or absolute ethical criteria of right and wrong (1951, p. 180).

Matter—in and of itself—is impotent to evolve any sense of moral consciousness. If there is no purpose in the Universe, as Simpson and others have asserted, then there is no purpose to morality or ethics. But the concept of a purposeless morality, or a purposeless ethic, is irrational. Unbelief therefore must contend, and, in fact, does contend, that there is no ultimate standard of moral/ethical truth, and that, at best, morality and ethics are relative and situational. [Morality is the character of being in accord with the principles or standards of right conduct. Ethics generally is viewed as the system or code by which attitudes and actions are determined to be either right or wrong.] That being the case, who could ever suggest (correctly) that someone else's conduct was "wrong," or that a man "ought" or "ought not" to do thus and so? The simple fact of the matter is that infidelity cannot explain the origin of morality and ethics. If there is no God, man exists in an environment where "anything goes." Russian novelist Fyodor Dostoevsky, in *The Brothers Karamazov* (1880), had one of his characters (Ivan) say that in the absence of God, everything is allowed. French existential philosopher Jean Paul Sartre later wrote:

> Everything is indeed permitted if God does not exist, and man is in consequence forlorn, for he cannot find anything to depend upon either within or outside himself.... Nor, on the other hand, if God does not exist, are we provided with any values or commands that could legitimize our behavior (1961, p. 485).

Sartre contended that **whatever** one chooses to do is right, and that value is attached to the choice itself so that "we can never choose evil" (1966, p. 279). Thus, it is impossible to formulate a system of ethics by which one objectively can differentiate "right" from "wrong." Agnostic British philosopher Bertrand Russell admitted as much when he wrote in his *Autobiography*:

> We feel that the man who brings widespread happiness at the expense of misery to himself is a better man than the man who brings unhappiness to others and happiness to himself. I do not know of any rational ground for this view, or, perhaps, for the somewhat more rational view that whatever the majority desires (called utilitarian hedonism) is preferable to what the minority desires. These are truly ethical problems but I do not know of any way in which they can be solved except by politics or war. All that I can find to say on this subject is that **an ethical opinion can only be defended by an ethical axiom, but, if the axiom is not accepted, there is no way of reaching a rational conclusion** (1969, 3:29, emp. added).

If there is no objective ethical axiom—no moral right or wrong—the concept of violating any kind of "law" becomes ludicrous, and punishment therefore would be futile. If no law or standard has been violated, with what justification may punishment then be enacted? Yet the concepts of moral right or wrong, and ethical obligation, are experienced by all men to a greater or lesser degree. Although Simpson argued that "man is the result of a purposeless and materialistic process that did not have him in mind," he was forced to admit that

[G]ood and evil, right and wrong, concepts irrelevant in nature except from the human viewpoint, become **real and pressing features** of the whole cosmos as viewed morally because **morals arise only in man** (1951, p. 179, emp. added).

Some have objected, of course, and have suggested that there are serious differences in various cultures regarding what is perceived as right and wrong. Charles Baylis, in an article on "Conscience" in *The Encyclopedia of Philosophy,* mentioned this objection and called attention to such differences as those between conscientious objectors to war versus volunteers, and cannibals versus vegetarians (1967, 1/2:190). This misses the point, however. C.S. Lewis observed that even though there may be differences between moralities, those differences have not "amounted to anything like a total difference" (1952, p. 19). They clearly would not, as Baylis suggested, "differ radically." As Lewis went on to remark, a totally different morality would consist of something like (to choose just two examples) a country where people were admired for running away from battle, or a person who felt proud for double-crossing those who had been kindest to him. Yet as Thomas C. Mayberry has noted: "There is broad agreement that lying, promise breaking, killing, and so on, are generally wrong" (1970, 154:113). Atheistic philosopher Kai Nielsen even admitted that to inquire, "Is murder evil?," is to ask a self-answering question (1973, p. 16). Why is this the case? In his book, *Does God Exist?*, A.E. Taylor wrote:

> But it is an undeniable fact that men do not merely love and procreate, they also hold that there is a difference between right and wrong; there are things which they **ought** to do and other things which they **ought not** to do. Different groups of men, living under different conditions and in different ages, may disagree widely on the question whether a certain thing belongs to the first or the second of these classes. They may draw the line between right and wrong in a different place, but at least they all agree that there is such a line to be drawn (1945, p. 83).

Paul wrote in Romans 2:14-15:

> For when the Gentiles, which have not the law, do by nature
> the things contained in the law, these, having not the law,
> are a law unto themselves: which show the work of the law
> written in their hearts, their conscience also bearing witness,
> and their thoughts meanwhile accusing or else excusing one
> another.

Although the Gentiles (unlike their Jewish counterparts) had no **written** law, they nevertheless had a law—a **moral** law—and they felt an obligation to live up to that law. Their conscience testified in regard to certain moral obligations in agreement with the law—urging them to do right and discouraging them from doing wrong.

But why was this the case? How is it that "morals arise only in man" and thus become "real and pressing features" of the Cosmos? Why did the Gentiles feel an obligation to uphold a certain ethical law? Who, or what, was the source of that law "written in their hearts"? The answer to such questions, of course, can be found only in the acknowledgment that the Creator of the Cosmos and the Author of that ethical law are one and the same—God!

Because of Who He is (Sovereign Creator), and because of what He has done (redeemed sinful man), He has the right to establish the moral/ethical laws that men are to follow, and to establish the punishment for any violation of those laws that might occur. I repeat: If there were no law, then there could be no sin—since where there is no objective standard there can be no right or wrong. If there is no sin, then there is no moral responsibility incumbent upon man. But if no moral responsibility is required of us, why, then, do we find courts and prisons spanning the globe?

Punishment for infractions of this moral/ethical code, however, can take any one of three forms—preventative, remedial, or retributive. Preventative punishment is a penalty exacted in order to deter others from acting in a similar unlawful fashion (e.g., soldiers who refused to obey a legitimate order from a superior officer being court-martialed). Remedial punishment is intended as a penalty to evoke improvement in the person(s) being punished (e.g., an employer requiring an employee to remain after his shift is over because of being a slacker on the job). Retributive punishment is a penalty meted out because, quite simply, it is deserved (e.g., a student being suspended from school for verbally abusing a teacher).

All three types of punishment are biblical in nature. Preventative punishment was evident in the deaths of Ananias and Sapphira after they lied about their donation to the church (Acts 5; note specifically verse 11: "And great fear came upon the whole church, and upon all that heard these things."). Remedial punishment can be observed in passages like Hebrews 12:6-7, where the writer told the saints:

> For whom the Lord loveth he chasteneth, and scourgeth every son whom he receiveth. It is for chastening that ye endure; God dealeth with you as with sons; for what son is there whom his father chasteneth not?

Retributive punishment is evident in God's instructions to Noah after the Flood: "Whoso sheddeth man's blood, by man shall his blood be shed, for in the image of God made he man." Granted, at times the various types of punishment may (and often do) overlap. Forcing disobedient soldiers to endure a court-martial, and then sending them to prison, not only will have a beneficial effect on others (preventative punishment), but hopefully will deter those who broke the law from ever doing so again (remedial punishment).

In employing retributive punishment, however, God will "pay back" the wicked. Paul, in referring to God's words in Leviticus 19: 18 and Deuteronomy 32:35, reminded the first-century Christians who were undergoing severe persecution: "'Vengeance is mine; I will repay,' saith the Lord" (Romans 12:19). In writing his second epistle to the Christians at Thessalonica, Paul assured them that God was just, and that

> It is a righteous thing with God to recompense affliction to them that afflict you, and to you that are afflicted rest with us,

at the revelation of the Lord Jesus from heaven with the angels of his power in flaming fire, rendering vengeance to them that know not God, and to them that obey not the gospel of our Lord Jesus: who shall suffer punishment, even eternal destruction from the face of the Lord and from the glory of his might (2 Thessalonians 1:6-9).

When the writer of the book of Hebrews cried out, "It is a fearful thing to fall into the hands of the living God" (10:31), he was attempting to warn us against having to endure the retributive punishment of God. The famous British preacher, Charles Spurgeon, once said:

When men talk of a little hell, it is because they think they have only a little sin, and they believe in a little Savior. But when you get a great sense of sin, you want a great Savior, and feel that if you do not have him, you will fall into a great destruction, and suffer a great punishment at the hands of the great God (as quoted in Carter, 1988, p. 36).

Those who suggest that no "good God" ever could condemn people's souls to eternal punishment obviously have failed to grasp the "great sense of sin" of which Spurgeon spoke. Nor do they understand the horrible price Heaven paid to offer sanctification, justification, and redemption to sinful mankind. As Paul stated the matter in Romans 5:10:

But God commendeth his own love toward us, in that, while we were yet sinners, Christ died for us. Much more then, being now justified by his blood, shall we be saved from the wrath of God through him. For if, while we were enemies, we were reconciled to God through the death of his Son, much more, being reconciled, shall we be saved by his life.

As Jesus hung on the cross dying for sins that He did not commit —in order to pay a debt that He did not owe, and a debt that we could not pay—He raised His voice and implored: "My God, my God, why hast thou forsaken me?" (Matthew 27:46). One writer described Christ's words as "among the most shocking in Scripture" (Peterson, 1995, p. 214). Why? The word "forsaken" is defined as to "abandon, desert," and is used here of "being forsaken by God"

(Bauer, et al., 1979, p. 215). Imagine the Son of God—abandoned, deserted, and forsaken **by His own Father** in order to pay the price for **our** sins!

Christ suffered the wrath of God so that mankind would not have to endure that wrath. In the Garden of Gethsemane, as Peter drew his sword to defend his Lord, Jesus turned to him and asked: "The cup which the Father hath given me, shall I not drink it?" (John 18: 11). What, exactly, was this "cup"? And why did it bring such anguish to Christ's soul? The Old Testament provides the answer. In Jeremiah 25:15ff., the weeping prophet wrote:

> For thus saith Jehovah, the God of Israel, unto me: "Take this cup of the wine of wrath at my hand, and cause all the nations, to whom I send thee, to drink it. And they shall drink, and reel to and fro, and be mad, because of the sword that I will send among them."

When the evil nations to whom Jeremiah spoke drank of the "cup of God's wrath," they were destroyed—never to rise again—because God's anger at their evil ways was so intense (vss. 26-27). The psalmist referred to the same cup of wrath when he wrote:

> But God is the judge: He putteth down one, and lifteth up another. For in the hand of Jehovah there is a cup, and the wine foameth; it is full of mixture, and he poureth out of the same. Surely the dregs thereof, all the wicked of the earth shall drain them, and drink them (75:7-9).

Peterson observed in regard to these two passages:

> This is the cup from which our holy Savior recoiled. A cup for "all the wicked of the earth" (Ps. 75:8), this cup, full of the wine of God's wrath (Jer. 25:15), should never have touched Jesus' sinless hands. That is why he was "overwhelmed with sorrow to the point of death" (Matt. 26:38) and prayed three times for the Father to take it away. On the cross the son of God drank to the dregs the cup of God's wrath for sinners like you and me.... And he did so willingly! (1995, p. 216).

At the cross, we catch a glimpse of the enormity of our sin and its offense to God. Christ—forsaken by His Father—suffered the retributive punishment that should have been ours. We deserved it; He did not. At the cross, we stare deeply into the vast chasm of human sin, and within it we see nothing but that which is vile and dark. But it is also at the cross where we stare deeply into the mysterious, unfathomable, incomprehensible love of God, and within it see a holy and righteous Sovereign Who, while abandoning and deserting His own Son, stubbornly refused to abandon and desert us. As Peterson went on to say:

> Viewed in the light of the Father's everlasting love for him, Jesus' cry of abandonment in Matthew 27:46 is almost impossible to understand. **The eternal relations between Father and Son were temporarily interrupted!** The preceding verse hints at this when it tells us that darkness covered the land of Israel from noon until 3 p.m.; **a profound judgment was taking place** (1995, p. 214, emp. added).

Elizabeth Browning set these eternal truths into poignant poetic form when she wrote:

> Yea, once Immanuel's orphaned cry his universe hath shaken.
> It went up single, echoless, "My God, I am forsaken!"
> It went up from the Holy's lips amid His lost creation,
> That, of the lost, no son should use those words of desolation.

Once again, I say: Those who claim not to understand how God could send sinful men into eternal punishment simply do not comprehend either the abominable, repulsive nature of man's rebellious crime against God or the inestimable, unspeakable price Heaven paid to redeem rebellious man from Satan's clutches. Guy Woods wrote:

> Those who would palliate the punishment or seek to shorten its duration by pointing to the love, long-suffering, and patience of God, ignore other attributes of deity, and disregard

the fact that his goodness is evidenced just as much in his characteristics of justice and truth as in his love and long-suffering. As a matter of fact, love and long-suffering are valid only when the principles of justice and truth are also operative in the divine government. To promise punishment and then to unilaterally cancel it is impossible to One who is not only the God of love but also the God of truth! He will not do so because he cannot do so, and maintain his character. God cannot impeach his own veracity, since "it is impossible for God to lie." (Hebrews 6:18.) Were he to cease to be just and truthful, he would cease to be good. The effort to emphasize some of the attributes of the great Jehovah to the neglect of others, or to array some against others, is to compromise the divine character (1985, 127[9]:278).

I must confess that in my most private and contemplative moments, I have reflected on the meaning and seriousness of the moving passage found in Hebrews 10:28-29.

A man that hath set at nought Moses' law dieth without compassion on the word of two or three witnesses. Of **how much sorer punishment**, think ye, shall he be judged worthy, **who hath trodden under foot the Son of God**, and hath counted the blood of the covenant wherewith he was sanctified an unholy thing, and hath done despite unto the Spirit of grace?

And in those same private, contemplative moments, I confess that I also have wondered (viewing this matter from what is, admittedly, a purely human standpoint—as the proud, earthly father of two precious, irreplaceable, sons): If I gave "only" one of **my** sons' lives (God had "only" one!) in order to save a wicked wretch who was my enemy in the first place—and that enemy then not only spurned the unique, exquisite, priceless gift of my son's blood, but mocked the supreme sacrifice that both my son and I had gone to such great lengths to make on his behalf—what kind of retributive punishment would **I** devise for such a one?

5

BIBLE TEACHING ON HELL

As one examines the various means through which men have attempted to circumvent the idea of the existence of hell, it is evident that there is no shortage of such theories. From universalism on the one hand to annihilationism on the other, men have done their best to disgorge the concept of eternal punishment from their minds. Some even have suggested that the only "hell" men experience is that of their own making here on Earth. Such a notion is standard fare in the vernacular of our day. For example, people speak of the fact that "war is hell." They complain that, as they endure the vicissitudes of life, they are "going through hell." John Benton noted:

> When people's personal lives go wrong, when they get caught up in bitterness and anger, when perhaps there is vicious language and even violence in the family home, we sometimes speak of people creating "hell on earth...." The psychological agony of guilt or the deep pain of bereavement are spoken of colloquially as being "like hell" (Benton, 1985, p. 42).

In his book, *Hell and Salvation*, Leslie Woodson observed: "The reference to man's hard lot in life as 'going through hell' has become so commonplace that the modern mind has satisfied itself with the assumption that hell is nothing more" (1973, p. 30).

Believe whatever we will, say whatever we please: the simple fact is that none of these descriptions fits the biblical description of hell. And certainly, Jesus never spoke of hell in such a fashion. When He warned us to "fear Him who is able to destroy both soul and body in hell" (Matthew 10:28) and spoke of those who "shall go away into **eternal** punishment" (Matthew 25:46), He was not referring to some sort of temporary earthly misery resulting from war, bereavement, or the like. Furthermore, the idea that "hell" is represented by whatever "pangs of guilt" we may experience from time to time during this life is a foolish assertion indeed. As one writer summarized the matter:

> [I]t is a well-known fact that the more one sins the more callous he may become until he has "seared his conscience as with a hot iron" (II Tim. 4:2). **If this theory is true then it follows that the righteous suffer greater punishment than the wicked**. A wicked person can destroy his "hell" by searing his conscience. However, a righteous man will be sensitive to sin and will feel the pangs of guilt when he sins. And, the more devout he is the more sensitive he is about sin. Again, **if this theory is true the worse a man is the less he will suffer**. To escape hell one simply would plunge himself into unrestrained sin and harden his heart. Obviously this doctrine is false (Ealey, 1984, p. 22, emp. added).

As the book of Job makes clear, on occasion the righteous do suffer terribly, while the wicked seem to prosper. At times, the psalmist even grew envious of the prosperity of the wicked, and wondered if it really was to his benefit to strive to be righteous (Psalm 73:2-5,12-14). Absolute justice is a rarity in the here and now, but is guaranteed at the Judgment yet to come (Matthew 25:31-46). We would do well to remember that the "Judge of all the Earth" **will** "do that which is right" (Genesis 18:25). We also should remember:

> It is significant that the most solemn utterances on this subject fall from the lips of Christ himself. In the New Testament as a whole there is a deep reserve on the nature of the punishment of the lost, though of course the act of final judgement is prominent. But with Christ himself the statements are much more explicit (Carson, 1978, p. 14).

The urgent question then becomes: What did Christ and His inspired writers teach regarding hell? What does the Bible say on this extremely important topic?

The word "hell" (which occurs 23 times in the King James Version of the Bible) translates three different terms from the Greek New Testament—*hades, tartaros,* and *géenna.* While each has a different meaning, on occasion the KJV translators chose to translate each as "hell." Was this an error on their part? Considering the way the word was used in 1611, no, it was not. Robert Taylor addressed this point when he wrote:

> Hell in 1611 referred to the place of the unseen, the place that was beyond human eyesight, the place that was covered. In that day men who covered roofs were called hellers—they put coverings on buildings or covered them (1985, p. 160).

According to Brown, "this was a correct rendering in 1611 because the word 'Hell' in Elizabethan English also meant an unseen place (e.g., Matthew 16:18; Luke 16:23; Acts 2:27,31; et al.)" [1999, p. 171].

The actual origin of the Greek *hades* (transliterated as hades in the English) is not well known. Some scholars have suggested that it derives from two roots: *a* (a negative prefix depicting "not") and *idein* (a word meaning "to see"). Thus, according to *Thayer's Greek-English Lexicon, hades* would evoke the idea of "not to be seen" (1958, p. 11). W.E. Vine advocated the view that *hades* meant "all receiving" (1991, p. 368). The exact meaning of the term, however, must be determined via an examination of the context in which it is used. *Hades* occurs eleven times in the Greek New Testament. On ten occasions (Matthew 11:23; 16:18; Luke 10:15; 16:23; Acts 2:27,31; Revelation 1:18; 6:8; 20:13-14) the KJV translates it as "hell." [In such occurrences, most recent versions (e.g., the ASV, NKJV, et al.) transliterate the Greek as "hades."] Once (1 Corinthians 15:55), *hades* is translated as "grave."

The Greek *tartaros* is the noun (translated into English via the Latin *tartarus*, cf. ASV footnote on 2 Peter 2:4) from which the verb *tartarosas* (aorist participle of *tartaroo*) derives. Ralph Earle observed that the term signified "the dark abode of the wicked dead" (1986, p. 447). Originally, it seems to have carried the idea of a "deep place"—a connotation that it retains in both Job 40:15 and 41:23 in the Septuagint. The Greek poet, Homer, wrote in his *Iliad* of "dark Tartarus...the deepest pit" (8.13). The word *tartaros* occurs only once in the Greek New Testament (2 Peter 2:4), where it is translated "hell" ("God spared not angels...but cast them down to hell"). In writing of this singular occurrence, R.C.H. Lenski remarked: "The verb does not occur elsewhere in the Bible; it is seldom found in other writings. The noun 'Tartarus' occurs three times in the LXX [Septuagint—BT], but there is no corresponding Hebrew term. The word is of pagan origin..." (1966, p. 310).

The Greek *géenna* is the predominant term used in the New Testament to depict hell. The word "represents the Aramaic expression *ge hinnom*, meaning 'Valley of Hinnom' (Neh. 11:30; cf. Josh. 15:8), and for this reason the word is commonly transliterated into English as *Gehenna*" (Workman, 1993, p. 496). Several sites have been suggested for the "valley of Hinnom" (or Valley of the Son of Hinnom, Vos, 1956, 2:1183; Earle, 1986, p. 447), but most authorities now believe that it was located on the south side of Jerusalem. In the Bible, the valley is mentioned first in Joshua 15:8. Centuries later, the apostates of Judah used it as a place to offer child sacrifices to the pagan god Molech (2 Chronicles 28:3; 33:6). When good king Josiah ascended the throne and overthrew idolatry, he "defiled" the place called Topheth (a name signifying something to be abhorred and spit upon) in the Valley of Hinnom (2 Kings 23:10). The valley came to be reviled for the evil that had occurred there, and eventually turned into a smoldering garbage dump that served the entire city of Jerusalem. Years later, it even was used as a potter's field (as is evident from the many rock tombs that are known to rest at its lower end). A perpetual fire was kept burning to prevent the spread of contagion, and worms and maggots performed their unseen, unsavory tasks amidst the debris and decay (see Morey, 1984, p. 87; cf. Foster, 1971, pp. 764-765). J. Arthur Hoyles graphically described the grisly goings-on:

> Here the fires burned day and night, destroying the garbage and putrefying the atmosphere from the smell of rotten flesh or decaying vegetation. In time of war the carcasses of vanquished enemies might mingle with the refuse, thus furnishing patriotic writers with a clue as to the destiny of their own persecutors. They were destined to be destroyed in the fires that were never quenched (1957, p. 118).

By the second century B.C., the term *géenna* began to appear in Jewish literature as a symbolic designation for the place of unending, eternal punishment of the wicked dead. As Gary Workman noted:

> It is natural, therefore, that when the New Testament opens *Gehenna* would be the primary term for hell. It is so recorded eleven times from the lips of Jesus and is also used once by James. It was not to the literal Valley of Hinnom outside Jerusalem that they referred, nor anything similar to it, but rather to "the *Gehenna* of fire" in a realm beyond the grave. Both Jewish and Christian historians confirm that the prevailing view of Jews at the time of Christ (except the Sadducees who denied even the resurrection) was that of eternal punishment for the wicked. And since Jesus never attempted to correct Pharisaic thinking on the duration of *Gehenna*, as he did with eschatological errors of the Sadducees (Matt. 22:29), this is weighty evidence for the meaning he intended to convey by his use of the term (1993, pp. 496-497).

The word *géenna* occurs twelve times in the Greek New Testament. In nine of these (Matthew 5:29-30; 10:28; 23:15,33; Mark 9:43, 45; Luke 12:5; James 3:6—KJV), it is translated as "hell." Three times (Matthew 5:22; 18:9; Mark 9:47—KJV) it is translated as "hell fire." David Stevens has pointed out: "It is also significant that eleven of the twelve times that the word *gehenna* is used, it is used by the Lord himself! Thus, it is evident that what we know about *gehenna*, we learn from the Lord himself" (1991, 7[3]:21).

There exists a diversity of views regarding the usage of these terms in Scripture. For example, some scholars have suggested that hades (or the Old Testament *sheol*) is a generic term for **the abode of the dead, whether good or evil**, while they await the final Judgment—a view with which I concur. Thus, hades is composed of two compartments: (1) the abode of the spirits of the righteous (known either as paradise—Luke 23:43, or Abraham's bosom—Luke 16:22); and (2) the abode of the spirits of the wicked (Tartarus—2 Peter 2:4, or "torment"—Luke 16:23) [Davidson, 1970, p. 694; Denham, 1998, p. 609; Harris, et al., 1980, 2:892; Jackson, 1998, 33[9]:34-35; Stevens, 1991, 7[3]:21; Thayer, 1958, p. 11; Zerr, 1952, p. 17].

On the other hand, some scholars suggest that hades should not be used as an umbrella term to refer to the general abode of the dead. Rather, they suggest that after death, there exists: (1) the grave for the physical body (*sheol*, physical abyss, physical hades); (2) the abode of the spirits of the righteous (paradise, Abraham's bosom, the "third heaven"); and (3) the abode of the spirits of the wicked (Tartarus, spiritual abyss, spiritual hades) [McCord, 1979, 96[4]:6]. Still others have advocated the belief that hades, gehenna, and Tartarus are synonyms representing exactly the same thing—"the place of all the damned" (Lenski, 1966, p. 310).

There is one thing, however, on which advocates of each position agree wholeheartedly, and on which the biblical text is crystal clear: after death and the Judgment, gehenna (hell) will be the ultimate, final abode of the spirits of the wicked. But what, exactly, will hell be like?

Hell is a Place of Punishment for Bodies and Souls of the Disobedient Wicked

The Scriptures speak with clarity and precision on the topic of hell as a place of punishment appointed for the disobedient wicked. In his Revelation, John spoke of the fact that Satan would be "cast into the lake of fire and brimstone" and "tormented day and night for ever and ever" (Revelation 20:10). But Satan is not the only one mentioned by John in that context. The "beast" and the "false prophet" also will suffer the same fate. Gary Workman observed that these two terms represent "humans spoken of collectively as allies of the devil. It is 'they'—all of them—who are tormented forever.... Whatever the fire will do for Satan and his demons, it will also do for humans who join them there" (1992, 23[3]:34). Workman therefore concluded:

> It is said that the lost will be "cast" (*ballo*) into hell (Matt. 5: 29) or into "the furnace of fire" (Matt 13:42; cf. 18:8-9) as a "prison" (Matt. 18:30). The devil will be "cast" into the lake of fire to be tormented (Rev. 20:10), and so will people who follow him (v. 15).... The compound word for "cast" is *ek-ballo*. Thus it is said that the wicked will be "cast out" (Luke 13:28) into outer darkness (Matt. 8:12; 22:13; 25:30). Does this mean snuffed out of existence? No, for if "cast forth" (Matt. 8:12) means annihilation, the same word translated "cast out" in reference to demons four verses later must also mean the same thing (v. 16). But Jesus did not annihilate demons; instead, he sent them away (v. 31). When the devil was "cast out" at the cross (John 12:31), was he annihilated? When he was "cast" into the abyss or bottomless pit (Rev. 20:3), did he cease to exist? No, and neither will the lost (1992, 23[3]:33).

The psalmist wrote by inspiration: "The wicked shall be turned into hell, and all the nations that forget God" (9:17). Jesus taught that at Judgment, the wicked will "depart" into punishment "prepared for the devil and his angels" (Matthew 25:41; cf. Matthew 25: 46 where Jesus employed the Greek term *kolasis,* which means punishment, torment, suffering, and chastisement [see Brown, 1999, p. 173]). When John described those who would join the devil in hell's horrible abyss, he referred to "the fearful, and unbelieving, and abominable, and murderers, and fornicators, and sorcerers, and idolaters, and liars" (Revelation 21:8). Paul said that those who inhabit hell with Satan will be those who "know not God" and who "obey not the gospel of Christ" (2 Thessalonians 1:7-9).

In discussing gehenna in the *International Standard Bible Encyclopedia*, Geerhardus Vos addressed the verses that deal with hell, and then stated: "In all of these it designates the place of eternal punishment of the wicked, generally in connection with the final judgment.... Both body and soul are cast into it" (1956, 2:1183). E.M. Zerr commented: "*Gehenna* is the lake of unquenchable fire into which the whole being of the wicked (body, soul and spirit) will be cast after the judgment" (1952, p. 17). Hell is indeed described as a place of punishment and suffering (Matthew 25:46; Revelation 14:11) that involves both body and soul (Matthew 10:28). It is a place of sorrow and trouble (Psalm 116:3), contempt and shame (Daniel 12:2), affliction (Jonah 2:2), and torment and anguish (Luke 16:23-24). It is a place of "outer darkness" (Matthew 8:12; 25:30) that Jude described as "blackness of darkness" (13) and that Peter referred to as "pits of darkness" (2 Peter 2:4) because those who inhabit it will be removed from the source of light (2 Thessalonians 1:9).

Hell is a Place of Conscious Sorrow, Torment, Pain, and Suffering

From such vivid descriptions, it is quite evident that the wicked will be in a state of **consciousness**. In fact, John wrote that Satan and his human cohorts would be "cast **alive** into the lake of fire that burneth with brimstone" (Revelation 19:20). That is to say, the Bible definitely teaches "**the persistence of personality** after physical death" (Warren, 1992, p. 32, emp. added). In addressing this point, Guy N. Woods offered the following assessment:

> If the Bible is a credible document—and of course it is—**conscious suffering is to be the lot of the wicked in the world to come**. The punishment the Righteous Judge will administer at that last great day is pain inflicted because of sin; it is inseparably associated with disobedience, and it is the action of the divine government for the violation of its laws. Some seek to soften the impact of the penalty by advancing the notion that the punishment threatened will be limited to remorse or con-

science, unhappy memories of neglected opportunities, hopelessness and despair. These are doubtless to be some of the **consequences** of eternal punishment, but not the **penalty**. One convicted of murder does not, by deep remorse from his horrible crime, thereby cancel the penalty which has fallen upon him because of his felonious act. He must still expiate his crime. (Romans 6:23.)

Many men and women today languish in lonely cells deeply regretful of their unsociable behavior and who would give the world to go back in time and cancel the act or acts which brought them to their present painful state. But bitter regrets alone will not discharge the debt they owe. A well-known warden of famous Sing-Sing prison many years ago wrote of walking slowly down the corridors of that formidable fortress at the midnight hour and of hearing the sobbing of distraught men separated from their loved ones and friends in the free world, some of whom would never enter it again (1985, 127[9]:278, first emp. added; last two in orig.).

When Christ described hell as a place of "weeping and gnashing of teeth" (Matthew 22:13), He overtly emphasized the fact that its inhabitants will endure **conscious** sorrow. Hell is a place of such terrible suffering (2 Thessalonians 1:9) that the apostle John referred to it as the "second death" (Revelation 20:14-15; 21:8). Benton summarized this well:

Hell is to be shut out from all joy, light and life. It is to be deprived of the good things you have tasted in life, but never appreciated. It is to be shut out of God's presence, cut off from all that is good and wholesome. It is to be cut off from all love, all peace, all joy for ever. Jesus explains that once people realize this, once they realize what they have missed, the effect upon them will be devastating. "There will be weeping and gnashing of teeth." It is an unspeakably sombre picture. Men seldom weep, but in hell men weep uncontrollably. Jesus speaks of the place being totally characterized by tears. The Greek in which the New Testament was written includes the definite article in Jesus' words. It is not just "weeping" in hell; it is "**the** weeping." It is as if Jesus is saying that every connotation of what is involved when people shed tears on earth is summed up in the total distress of hell. All the tears of earth are just a preview to the sobs of hell. Here, in this life, men and women weep, but **the** weeping awaits.... In hell people do not just weep; they gnash their teeth. Having been shut out of the presence of God into the eternal blackness, permanently deprived of all that is wholesome and good, in bitter anger men and women grind their teeth in speechless rage. As they realize that once and for all, "I've been shut out!" they are overcome with a sense of eternal loss which leads to a depth of anger and fury that they find impossible to express in words. What an awful picture is contained in the words of Jesus! (1985, pp. 47-48, emp. in orig.).

In addressing the consciousness of those in hell, Wayne Jackson wrote:

Punishment implies **consciousness**. It would be absurd to describe those who no longer exist as being "punished." The wicked will be "tormented" with the fire of Gehenna (cf. Rev. 14:10-11). Torment certainly implies awareness (cf. Rev. 9: 5; 11:10) [1998, 33[9]:35, emp. in orig.].

And torment there will be! When, in Revelation 20:10, John wrote of this torment, he employed the Greek word *basanisthesontai*, the root of which (*basanizo*) literally means "to torment, to be harassed, to torture, to vex with grievous pains" (Thayer, 1958, p. 96; cf. Matthew 8:6 regarding the one "tormented" [*basanizomenos*] with palsy).

Previously, John spoke of those who inhabit hell as experiencing the "wine of the wrath of God, which is prepared unmixed in the cup of his anger" (Revelation 14:10). Imagine—experiencing the undiluted wrath of God! In the next verse, John lamented: "The smoke of their torment [notice: **not** the smoke of their annihilation!—BT] goeth up for ever and ever." Little wonder, then, that the writer of Hebrews referred to the second death as "a sorer punishment" than any mere physical death (10:29).

Hell is a Place of Unquenchable
Fire and Undying Worms

Earlier I made the point that eleven of the twelve times where the word gehenna is employed in the New Testament, it was Christ Who was doing the speaking. In one of those instances (Mark 9: 43) He spoke of it as "unquenchable fire" (Greek *asbestos*—denoting something that cannot be extinguished; see Bagster, 1970, p. 54), and then five verses later described hell as a place "where their worm dieth not" (v. 48). In his *Greek-English Lexicon*, Joseph Thayer described fire as a metaphor for "the extreme penal torments, which the wicked are to undergo after their life on earth" (1958, p. 558). Gary Workman suggested:

> This double metaphor, used originally of temporal punishments in Isaiah 66:24, was used by Jesus to describe the future punishment in resurrection bodies. God once intervened with the laws of nature so that a bush "burned" (Ex. 3:2) but was "not burnt" (v. 3, same Hebrew word—*ba'ar*). Though it was on fire, it was "not consumed" (v. 2). In like manner God will suspend the natural laws of the temporal realm when people enter the eternal realm. Shadrach, Meshach and Abednego walked around in a fiery furnace without being burned up by the flames that consumed their enemies because God arranged for the fire to have "no power upon their bodies" (v. 27). In eternity God will arrange for the wicked to burn in the flames of hell while continuing to exist, just as they do right now in Hades (Luke 16:19-31). Their fate will be "everlasting burnings" (Isa. 33:14).... Our Lord could not have indicated an eternity of torment any clearer. The isolation and the fire did not **stop** their agony, but **caused** it (1992, 23[3]:31, emp. in orig.).

The second part of the metaphor used by the Lord concerned the fact that in hell "their worm (Greek, *skolex*, depicting a creature that feeds on dead animal or human remains) dieth not"—a fitting description in light of the fact that the Valley of Hinnom outside Jerusalem was well known for the flesh-eating maggots that feasted daily upon the rotting refuse of that eerie, other-worldly place. In their *Greek-English Lexicon*, Arndt and Gingrich remarked that the never-dying worm is used as a symbol of the unending "torment of the damned" (1957, p. 765). Greek scholar A.T. Robertson said that the phrase "is thus a vivid picture of eternal punishment" (1930, 1:346). Thayer recorded that the phrase referred to the fact that "their punishment after death will never cease" (1958, p. 580). Did the Lord mean what He said? Oh yes—He meant that, and more! As John Benton commented:

> This is a picture which suggests that in hell there is an eternal dissolution which never ceases.... Perhaps the nearest illustration we can use from our present experience is that of a sleepless night caused by worry. There is something upon your mind that causes you deep anxiety. The prospect of it scares you and drains you of all energy. The worry gets you nowhere and yet you cannot stop worrying about it. You feel as if you are falling apart as a person. You cannot be at peace or feel settled in yourself. It is as if something just keeps gnawing and gnawing away at you, something with which you just cannot come to terms. Jesus, with a love in his heart, does not want us to go there, warns us of the place where the "worm does not die." Hell is a place with which no one will ever be able to come to terms....
>
> The description of hell which emerges from Jesus' teaching is fearful. It is the most horrendous thing we can ever imagine. Knowing the character of Jesus, we cannot for a moment suppose that he merely intended to play upon people's fears in telling us such things. If Jesus was ignorant upon these profound subjects he had no right to set out such a dreadful picture to torment people's imaginations. Still less would he be justified in telling us such things if, being perfectly aware of the true nature of life after death, he knew that there was no such place as hell. It will not do to think that Jesus was using the ends to justify the means—to paint a terrible picture of hell simply in order to scare people into living a moral life, or into believing in him as a Saviour. **Jesus was not that kind of man**. Jesus was always a man of love and truth. He would not set out a picture if he had not been completely sure of it and he certainly would not tell lies. **Knowing the character**

of Jesus, we have got to say that he was simply being straight with us.... Jesus said in the Sermon on the Mount: "You have heard that it was said..but I tell you...." Jesus saw the consequences of sin as terrifying. He saw sin as leading people to this place of indescribable misery and so again he is shockingly urgent and direct in his warnings" (1985, pp. 55-56,51, emp. added).

In His account of the rich man and Lazarus in Luke 16, the Lord employed the vivid imagery of fire when He depicted the rich man as begging for relief because he was in agony in its clutches (vss. 23-24). Benton went on to state:

> [W]e must reject the idea that because it is picture language, it holds no meaning and no fear for us. Let nobody think that it is only symbolical and therefore not so terrible. Rather, we should realize that **if the symbol, the mere picture, is already awe-inspiring, how horrible must the actual reality be!** Surely, if anything is clear, it is that Jesus does not want us to toy with the possibility that hell might be bearable. A symbol representing something is never greater than the thing itself (1985, p. 52, emp. added).

Those who attempt to portray the account in Luke 16 as merely allegorical or metaphorical are wasting their considerable efforts. As John Blanchard has reminded us: "In common communication the thing being symbolized is always greater than the symbol.... [E]ven if we can prove that hell's 'fire' and 'worm' are metaphorical we shall not have removed one iota of their horror or terror" (1993, p. 141). While considering the Lord's comments in Luke 16, Wayne Jackson asked: "If the condition of the rich man in hades was one of 'anguish' (*odunao*—'to suffer pain'), though it involved only the soul, does it seem likely that the ultimate punishment of Gehenna, which involves both body and soul, would entail **less**?" (1998, 33[9]:35, emp. in orig.). Surely it was this very point that the Lord was attempting to emphasize to His hearers. Who—in their right mind—would go **voluntarily** to a fiery place of punishment, sorrow, torment, pain, and suffering that they knew was best described as one where "the [flesh-eating] worm dieth not"?

Hell is Eternal in Nature

Surely, one of the most horrific aspects of hell is its eternal nature. Throughout the Bible, words like "eternal," "forever and forever," "unquenchable," and "everlasting" are used repeatedly to describe the duration of the punishment that God will inflict upon the wicked. Some, of course, have objected that "eternal" punishment simply is not acceptable since, on the face of it, it is "too long." Gary Ealey responded to such an objection when he wrote:

> If it is argued that "everlasting" punishment is too long or severe, we again reply that such a conclusion is based upon our inability to fully appreciate the ugliness of sin. How do you determine the hideousness of an act? Do you do so on the basis of the time involved in performing the act itself? If a man in a football stadium filled with people fired a machine gun for thirty seconds and kills 100 people, should he be punished for 100 seconds? Would you double that? Triple it? Would you sentence him to life imprisonment or to execution? Clearly, only God can determine what is the just punishment for sin (1984, p. 25).

As the "Judge of all the earth" (Genesis 18:25), God alone has the right to determine the nature and duration of whatever punishment is due to the wicked. And He has decreed that such punishment will be eternal in nature (Matthew 25:46; Revelation 14:10-11). That mighty not agree with our mind-set, or appeal to our sensitivities, but it is God's word on the matter nevertheless.

I once heard of a newspaper in Detroit, Michigan that published a story about a man who (ironically) had been transferred from Hell, Michigan to a city by the name of Paradise. The headline read: "Man Leaves Hell for Paradise!" Such an event might occur in **this** lifetime, but you may rest assured that it will not happen in the **next** (Luke 16:19-31). When Dante, in his *Inferno*, depicted the sign hanging over hell's door as reading, "Abandon all hope, ye who enter here," he did not overstate the case.

Others have objected to the concept of **eternal** punishment because of such passages as Mark 12:9 (where Jesus foretold in a parable that God would "destroy" those who killed His beloved Son) and Matthew 10:28 (where Jesus told His disciples to fear Him who was able to "destroy" both soul and body in hell). But the belief that the soul will be annihilated is based, not on an understanding, but on a **mis**understanding, of the passages in question. In addition to referring to destruction, the Greek word *apollumi* employed in these two portions of Scripture (and approximately 90 more times elsewhere in the New Testament) also can mean "lose," "perish," or "lost." As Vine pointed out: "The idea is not extinction but ruin, loss, not of being, but of well-being" (1991, p. 211). Thayer defined *apollumi* as it appears in Matthew 10:28 as "to devote or give over to eternal misery" (1958, p. 64). In speaking of the idea of eternal punishment as expressed in Matthew 25:46, Adam Clarke wrote:

> But some are of opinion that this punishment shall have an end: this is as like as that the glory of the righteous shall have **an end**: for the same word is used to express the **duration** of the punishment, *kolasin aionion*, as is used to express the duration of the state of glory: *zoen aionion*. I have seen the best things written in favour of the final redemption of damned spirits; but I never saw an answer to the argument against that doctrine, drawn from this verse, but what sound learning and criticism should be ashamed to acknowledge. The original word *aion* is certainly to be taken here in its proper grammatical sense, **continued being**, *aieion*, **never ending**. Some have gone a **middle** way, and think that the wicked shall be **annihilated**. This, I think, is contrary to the text; if they go **into punishment**, they **continue** to **exist**; for that which **ceases** to **be**, **ceases** to **suffer** (n.d., 5:244, emp. in orig.).

Granted, it would be more comforting for the wicked to believe that at the end of this life they simply will be punished "for a little while" and then "drop out of existence," rather than having to face the stark realization of an eternal punishment in the fires of hell. But comforting or not, the question must be asked: Is such a belief in compliance with biblical teaching on this subject?

While it is true that, on rare occasions in Scripture, words such as "everlasting" and "forever" may be used in a non-literal sense (i.e., the thing being discussed is not strictly eternal—e.g. Exodus 12:14 and Numbers 25:13), they **never** are used in such a sense when describing hell. The word *aionios* occurs some seventy times in the Greek New Testament where it is translated by such English terms as "eternal" or "everlasting" (e.g., "eternal fire," Matthew 18: 8, 25:41, Jude 7; "eternal punishment," Matthew 25:46; "eternal destruction," 2 Thessalonians 1:9; and "eternal judgment," Hebrews 6:2). In his *Expository Dictionary of New Testament Words,* Vine wrote of *aionios*:

> Moreover, it is used of persons and things which are in their nature, endless, as, e.g., of God (Rom 16:26); of His power (I Tim. 6:16), and of Him (I Peter 5:10); of the Holy Spirit (Heb. 9:14); of the redemption effected by Christ (Heb. 9:12), and of the consequent salvation of men (5:9); ...and of the resurrection body (II Cor. 5:1), elsewhere said to be "immortal" (I Cor. 15:53), in which that life will be finally realized (Matt. 25:46; Titus 1:2) [1966, p. 43].

Thayer stated that *aionios* means "without end, never to cease, everlasting" (1958, p. 112).

In his inspired discussion about the coming fate of false teachers, Jude assured the first-century Christians that those who perverted the truth **would** be punished. To illustrate his point, he reached back to Sodom and Gomorrah (Genesis 19:24-25) as an example of those "suffering the punishment of eternal fire" (v. 7). G.L. Lawlor commented on Jude's illustration as follows:

> Jude says these cities, their sin, and their terrible destruction lie before us as an example, *deigma.* Better, perhaps, the word might be rendered "sign," that is, to show us the meaning and significance of something, i.e., this awful sin and God's catastrophic judgment. The cities were destroyed by fire and brimstone, but the ungodly inhabitants are even now undergoing the awful torment of everlasting punishment. These cities are an example, they lie before us as a sign, to show the certainty of divine punishment upon an apostasy of life dreadful almost beyond description (1972, p. 70).

But what did Lawlor mean when he said that the inhabitants of Sodom and Gomorrah "are even now undergoing the awful torment of everlasting punishment"? His point is this. The Greek *hupechousai* (rendered "suffering") is a present participle which "shows that they were enduring 'eternal fire' even as Jude wrote! The primary force of the present tense in the Greek, especially as connected with a participial construction as here, is that of **continuous** action" (Denham, 1998, p. 607, emp. added). Greek scholar M.R. Vincent wrote regarding this point: "The participle is present, indicating that they are suffering to this day the punishment which came upon them in Lot's time" (1946, 1:340). Brown remarked: "This grammatical construction simply means that Jude is saying that the inhabitants of the two cities not only suffered, but they continue to suffer. What a warning to those in rebellion to God!" (1999, p. 176).

The Jews (and Jewish Christians) of Jude's day would have understood that point because they knew and understood the significance attached to gehenna. Alfred Edersheim, who stood without equal as a Hebrew/intertestamental period scholar, devoted an entire chapter of his monumental work, *The Life and Times of Jesus the Messiah*, to the rabbinical and New Testament evidence on the subject of eternal punishment. His conclusion was that the Jews in the time of Christ understood gehenna as referring to a place of eternal, conscious torment for the wicked (1971, pp. 791-796). Eminent religious historian Phillip Schaff (1970, 2:136) reported that, except for the Sadducees (who believed in neither a resurrection for the righteous nor the wicked), the Jews of Christ's day consistently held to a view of personal, eternal, conscious punishment —a truly important point for the following reason.

During His ministry, Jesus was quite outspoken against those things that were wrong or misleading. In Matthew 22:23-33 He chastised the Sadducees severely regarding their erroneous views about the lack of a future existence. Yet, as noted earlier, He **never opposed** the Jewish concept of eternal punishment of the soul. Had the Jews been in error regarding the afterlife, surely the Son of God would have corrected them in as public a manner as He did on so many other points of Scripture. Instead, He **repeatedly reaffirmed** such a concept. His silence speaks volumes!

No Hell...No Heaven

When Christ spoke to the people of His day about the ultimate fate of humanity in eternity, He stated that the wicked would "go away into everlasting (*aionios*) punishment, but the righteous into eternal (*aionios*) life." As Denham has pointed out: "The word rendered 'eternal' is the same Greek word *aionios*, rendered earlier as 'everlasting'" (1998, p. 615). The Lord's double use of the term *aionios* is critically important in this discussion. J.W. McGarvey addressed this fact when he wrote:

> Whatever this Greek word means in the last clause of this sentence it means in the first; for it is an invariable rule of exegesis, that a word when thus repeated in the same sentence must be understood in the same sense, unless the context or the nature of the subject shows that there is a play on the word. There is certainly nothing in the context to indicate the slightest difference in meaning, nor can we know by the nature of the subject that the punishment spoken of is less durable than the life. It is admitted on all hands that in the expression "everlasting life" the term has its full force, and therefore it is idle and preposterous to deny that it has the same force in the expression "everlasting punishment." The everlasting punishment is the same as the everlasting fire of verse 41. The punishment is by fire, and its duration is eternal (1875, pp. 221-222).

There can be absolutely no doubt that the Lord intended to teach two specific states of conscious future existence. In fact, as James Orr observed in the *International Standard Bible Encyclopedia:* "The whole doctrine of the future judgment in the NT presupposes survival after death" (1956, 4:2502). Writing in *The New International Dictionary of New Testament Theology*, Joachim

Guhrt stated that since "God's life never ends, i.e., that everything belonging to him can also never come to an end,...even perdition must be called *aionios*, eternal" (1978, pp. 830,833). In this same vein, Guy N. Woods commented: "Our heavenly Father is described as 'the everlasting God.' (Romans 16:26.) Hell will be the inhabitation of the wicked so long as God himself exists" (1985, 127[9]: 278). George Ladd thus noted:

> The adjective *aionios* does not of itself carry a qualitative significance, designating a life that is different in kind from human life. The primary meaning of the word is temporal. It is used of fire, punishment, sin, and places of abode; and these uses designate **unending duration** (1974, p. 255, emp. added).

But that is only half of the Lord's message. Orr went on to say: "Here precisely the same word is applied to the punishment of the wicked **as to the blessedness of the righteous**.... Whatever else the term includes, it connotes duration" (1956, 4:2502, emp. added). When he discussed the definition and meaning of the word *aionios* in *The Theological Dictionary of the New Testament,* Herman Sasse noted that when the word is used "as a term for eschatological expectation," if it conveys "eternity" for the rewards of the righteous it also must convey "the sense of 'unceasing' or 'endless'" (1964, 1:209). Therefore, "however long then the righteous will experience the blessedness of **eternal** life is just how long the wicked will suffer **everlasting** punishment..." (Denham, 1998, p. 615, emp. in orig.).

In his intriguing book, *Hell on Trial—The Case for Eternal Punishment,* Robert Peterson wrote the following under the chapter titled "The Case for Eternal Punishment": "Jesus places the fates of the wicked and the righteous side by side.... The parallelism makes the meaning unmistakable: the punishment of the ungodly and the bliss of the godly both last forever" (1995, p. 196). Gary Workman spoke to this very point when he observed:

New Testament writers used *aion* and *aionios* 141 times when speaking of eternity to convey the idea of unceasing, endless, and perpetual. If the word means "without end" when applied to the future blessedness of the saved, it must also mean "without end" when describing the future punishment of the lost (1992, 23[3]:33).

Benton elaborated:

> The same word *aionios*, "eternal," is used to describe both heaven and hell. If we take the position that hell is capable of termination then, to be consistent, we must believe that the same is true of heaven. But, from the rest of the Bible, that is plainly not the case. Heaven is **for ever**. We must stay with the plain meaning of the word "eternal." Both heaven and hell are without end (1985, p. 55, emp. in orig.).

These writers are correct. The fact that Christ made a special point of repeating *aionios* in the same sentence requires that we "stay with the plain meaning of the word." Hoekema therefore concluded:

> The word *aionios* means without end when applied to the future blessedness of believers. It must follow, unless clear evidence is given to the contrary, that this word also means without end when used to describe the future punishment of the lost.... It follows, then, that the punishment which the lost will suffer after this life will be as endless as the future happiness of the people of God (1982, p. 270).

Those who argue against an eternal hell must be provided with teaching to help them realize that whatever arguments they make against the eternal abode of the wicked apply with equal force to the eternal abode of the righteous. Perhaps it is the realization of the unscriptural implications of such a position that elicits such righteous indignation on the part of those who accept Christ's instruction on the nature of eternity—because they realize that suggestions intended to limit the nature of hell have a correspondingly similar effect on heaven. For example, two short years after Edward Fudge published his book, *The Fire That Consumes* (in which he advocated the doctrine of annihilationism), Robert Morey published *Death and the*

Afterlife, a scholarly refutation of Fudge's position that one writer suggested was so well argued that it "took Fudge to the theological woodshed" (Jackson, 1993, p. 64). Later, theologian John Gerstner authored *Repent or Perish*, a huge portion of which also was devoted to examining and refuting Fudge's arguments. [Interestingly, in his book Gerstner suggested that the masterful manner in which Morey demolished Fudge's arguments might be compared to using a battlefield canon to kill a housefly! (1990, p. 41).]

Those who are willing to accept Christ's teaching on heaven should have no trouble accepting His teaching on hell. Yet some do. Their refusal to accept biblical teaching on the eternal nature of the wicked, however, is not without consequences. John Benton accurately summarized the situation.

> Disregarding the doctrine of eternal damnation tends to make us doubt eternal salvation.... Though Revelation 21-22 proclaims the final fate of the wicked—existence in the lake of fire (21:8) and exclusion from the city of God (22:15)—these chapters trumpet more loudly the final destiny of the redeemed (1995, p. 217).

But does it **really** matter **what** a person believes in this regard? Wayne Jackson answered that question when he wrote: "Those who contend that the wicked will be annihilated are in error. But is the issue one of importance? Yes. **Any theory of divine retribution which undermines the full consequences of rebelling against God has to be most dangerous**" (1998, 33[9]:35, emp. added).

Since both heaven and hell are described via the same, exact terminology in Scripture, once the instruction of the Lord and His inspired writers on the subject of an eternal hell has been abandoned, how long will it be before the Bible's instruction on the eternal nature of heaven likewise is abandoned? Have we not witnessed the effects of this type of thinking before? Those who started out to compromise the first chapter of Genesis eventually compromised other important facets of biblical doctrine as well (e.g., biblical miracles, Christ's virgin birth, the Lord's bodily resurrection, etc.). For many, rejecting the biblical concept of the eternality of hell may well represent the first steps on the slippery slope that eventually will lead to compromise in other areas of Scripture. Surely it would be better by far to echo the heartfelt sentiments of Joshua when he told the Israelites that while they were free to believe whatever they wished, or to act in any manner they chose, "as for me and my house, we will serve Jehovah" (Joshua 24:15).

6
CONCLUSION

The latter part of this book has dealt at some length with the concept of the souls of the wicked inhabiting an eternal hell, but has had relatively little to say about the concept of the souls of the righteous inhabiting an eternal heaven. Actually, this should not be all that surprising. The very idea of hell has met with violent opposition—for good reason. No one **wants** to go to hell. Thus, the Good Book's teaching on heaven is accepted far more readily than its teaching on hell.

The simple fact of the matter, however, is that God created man as a dichotomous being who consists of both a body and a soul. When eventually each of us has "shuffled off this **mortal** coil" (to quote Shakespeare), our **immortal** soul will return to God Who gave it (Ecclesiastes 12:7). Infidelity, of course, always has objected strenuously to the concept of "life after death." The very idea seems preposterous to unbelievers—just as it did to King Agrippa in the first century when Paul asked the pagan monarch: "Why is it judged incredible with you, if God doth raise the dead?" (Acts 26:28).

Indeed, why should it be difficult to believe that an omnipotent God could raise the dead? For the God Who created the Universe and everything within it in six days, and Who upholds "all things by the word of his power" (Hebrews 1:3), how difficult could it be to raise the dead? As Blaise Pascal, the famed French philosopher once remarked: "I see no greater difficulty in believing the resurrection of the dead than the creation of the world. Is it less easy to reproduce a human body than it was to produce it at first?" (as quoted in Otten, 1988, p. 40). In commenting on this point, Herman J. Otten, long-time editor of *Christian News*, wrote: "The task will not be ours. Omnipotence and omniscience have assumed it; they will do it, and they will do it well" (1988, p. 40).

Indeed, God will do His part well. Writing in the book of Revelation, the apostle John described in unforgettable language the destiny of the righteous when this world finally comes to an end: "Behold, the dwelling of God is with men. He will dwell with them, and they shall be his people, and God himself will be with them" (21:3, RSV). Thousands of years earlier, God's pledge to Abraham had foreshadowed just such a covenant relationship. Moses recorded: "And I will establish My covenant between Me and you and your descendants after you in their generations, for an everlasting covenant, to be God to you and your descendants after you" (Genesis 17:7, NKJV). Paul spoke of the fact that "if ye are Christ's, then are ye Abraham's seed, heirs according to promise" (Galatians 3:29), and referred to those who serve Christ faithfully as "heirs according to the hope of eternal life" (Titus 3:7). James rejoiced in the fact that those who were "rich in faith" would be "heirs of the kingdom that he promised to them who love him" (James 2:5). The writer of the book of Hebrews spoke of Christ as having become "unto all them that obey him, the author of eternal salvation" (5:9).

No doubt that is exactly what John had in mind when he went on to say in Revelation 21: "He that overcometh shall inherit these things; and I will be his God, and he shall be my son" (vs. 7). God will be Father to the man or woman who demonstrates faith in Him, perseveres to the end, and lives in humble obedience to His divine will. Such is the promise of sonship to believers. God will welcome those who believe in and obey His Son as "heirs of God, and joint-heirs with Christ" (Romans 8:17), and will—according to His promise—bestow upon them all the riches and blessings of heaven.

In the next verse, however, John went on to paint a picture of stark contrast when he described the ultimate end of the impenitent wicked:

> But for the fearful, and unbelieving, and abominable, and murderers, and fornicators, and sorcerers, and idolaters, and all liars, their part shall be in the lake that burneth with fire and brimstone; which is the second death (Revelation 21:8).

What diametric alternatives—enjoying eternal happiness as a son or daughter of God, or enduring eternal pain in "the lake that burneth with fire and brimstone"!

The good news, of course, is that no one **has** to go to hell. When Christ was ransomed on our behalf (1 Timothy 2:4), He paid a debt He did not owe, and a debt we could not pay, so that we could live forever in the presence of our Creator (Matthew 25:46). God takes no joy at the death of the wicked (Ezekiel 18:23; 33:11). Nor should we. As one writer eloquently stated it: "No one who has been snatched from the burning himself can feel anything but compassion and concern for the lost" (Woodson, 1973, p. 32).

As we begin to comprehend both the hideous nature of our sin, and the alienation from God resulting from it, we not only should exhibit a fervent desire to save ourselves "from this crooked generation" (Acts 2:40), but we also should feel just as passionate about warning the wicked of their impending doom (Ezekiel 3:17-19).

REFERENCES

Arndt, William and F.W. Gingrich (1957), *A Greek-English Lexicon of the New Testament and Other Early Christian Literature* (Chicago, IL: University of Chicago Press).

Barclay, William (1967), *The Plain Man Looks at the Apostles' Creed* (London: Collins).

Bauer, W., W.F. Arndt, F.W. Gingrich, and F. Danker (1979), *A Greek Lexicon of the New Testament and Other Early Christian Literature* (Chicago, IL: University of Chicago Press).

Baylis, Charles (1967), "Conscience," *The Encyclopedia of Philosophy*, ed. Paul Edwards (New York: Macmillan), 1/2:189-191.

Benton, John (1985), *How Can a God of Love Send People to Hell?* (Welwyn, Hertfordshire, England: Evangelical Press).

Brown, David P. (1999), "Annihilation in Hell Error," *God Hath Spoken Affirming Truth and Reproving Error*, ed. Curtis Cates (Memphis, TN: Memphis School of Preaching), pp. 161-178.

Brown, Francis, S.R. Driver, and Charles Briggs (1907), *A Hebrew and English Lexicon of the Old Testament* (London: Oxford University Press).

Brunner, Emil (1954), *Eternal Hope* (Philadelphia, PA: Westminster).

Carson, Herbert M. (1978), *The Biblical Doctrine of Eternal Punishment*, Carey Conference Paper.

Carter, Tom (1988), *Spurgeon at His Best* (Grand Rapids, MI: Baker).

Clayton, John (1990a), "Book Reviews," *Does God Exist?*, 17[5]:20-21, September/October.

Clayton, John (1990b), *The Source: Eternal Design or Infinite Accident?* (South Bend, IN: Privately published by author).

Clayton, John (1991), *Does God Exist? Christian Evidences Intermediate Course Teacher's Guide* (South Bend, IN: Privately published by author).

Davidson, Benjamin (1970 reprint), *The Analytical Hebrew and Chaldee Lexicon* (Grand Rapids, MI: Zondervan).

Denham, Daniel (1998), "Will the Wicked Really be Punished with Eternal Fire?," *Studies in 1,2 Peter and Jude,* ed. Dub McClish (Denton, TX: Valid Publications), pp. 601-627.

Ealey, Gary (1984), "The Biblical Doctrine of Hell," *The Biblical Doctrine of Last Things,* ed. David L. Lipe (Kosciusko, MS: Magnolia Bible College), pp. 20-28.

Earle, Ralph (1986), *Word Meanings in the New Testament* (Grand Rapids, MI: Baker).

Edersheim, Alfred (1971 reprint), *The Life and Times of Jesus the Messiah* (Grand Rapids, MI: Eerdmans).

Ferguson, Jesse B. (1852), *Christian Magazine,* July.

Ferguson, Kitty (1994), *The Fire in the Equations: Science, Religion, and the Search for God* (Grand Rapids, MI: Eerdmans).

Flew, Antony G.N. and Thomas B. Warren (1977), *Warren-Flew Debate* (Jonesboro, AR: National Christian Press).

Foster, R.C. (1971 reprint), *Studies in the Life of Christ* (Grand Rapids, MI: Baker).

Fudge, Edward W. (1982), *The Fire That Consumes* (Houston, TX: Providential Press).

Gesenius, William (1979 reprint), *Hebrew-Chaldee Lexicon to the Old Testament* (Grand Rapids, MI: Baker).

Guhrt, Joachim (1978), "Time," *The New International Dictionary of New Testament Theology,* ed. Colin Brown (Grand Rapids, MI: Zondervan).

Harris, R.L., G.L. Archer, Jr., and B.K. Waltke (1980), *Theological Wordbook of the Old Testament* (Chicago, IL: Moody).

Henry, Carl F.H. (1967), *Evangelicals at the Brink of Crisis: Significance of the World Congress on Evangelism* (Waco, TX: Word).

Hoekema, Anthony (1982), *The Bible and the Future* (Grand Rapids, MI: Eerdmans).

Hoekema, Anthony (1986), *Created in God's Image* (Grand Rapids, MI: Eerdmans).

Hoyles, Arthur J. (1957), "The Punishment of the Wicked after Death," *London Quarterly and Holborn Review,* April.

Jackson, Wayne (1987), "Debate Challenge Withdrawn," *Christian Courier*, 23[8]:31, December.

Jackson, Wayne (1991), "The Origin and Nature of the Soul," *Christian Courier*, 27[5]:19, September.

Jackson, Wayne (1993), "Changing Attitudes Toward Hell," *Whatever Happened to Heaven and Hell?*, ed. Terry E. Hightower (San Antonio, TX: Shenandoah Church of Christ), pp. 63-67.

Jackson, Wayne (1998), "The Use of 'Hell' in the New Testament," *Christian Courier*, 33[9]:34-35, January.

Jastrow, Robert (1982), "A Scientist Caught Between Two Faiths," Interview with Bill Durbin, *Christianity Today,* August 6.

Ladd, George Eldon (1974), *A Theology of the New Testament* (Grand Rapids, MI: Eerdmans).

Lake, D.M. (1976), *Zondervan Pictorial Encyclopedia of the Bible*, ed. Merrill C. Tenney (Grand Rapids, MI: Zondervan).

Lawlor, George Lawrence (1972), *The Epistle of Jude* (Nutley, NJ: Presbyterian and Reformed).

Lenski, R.C.H. (1966), *The Interpretation of I and II Epistles of Peter, the Three Epistles of John, and the Epistle of Jude* (Minneapolis, MN: Augsburg).

Lewis, C.S. (1952), *Mere Christianity* (New York: Macmillan).

Lewis, C.S. (1966), *Letters to Malcolm, Chiefly on Prayer* (London: Fontana Books).

Lewis, Jack P. (1988), "Living Soul," *Exegesis of Difficult Passages* (Searcy, AR: Resource Publications).

Lewis, Joseph (1983), *Ingersoll the Magnificent* (Austin, TX: American Atheist Press).

Marais, J.L. (1956), "Spirit," *International Standard Bible Encyclopedia*, ed. James Orr (Grand Rapids, MI: Eerdmans), 5:2837-2838.

Mayberry, Thomas C. (1970), "God and Moral Authority," *The Monist*, January.

McCord, Hugo (1979), "The State of the Dead," *Firm Foundation*, 96[4]: 6,12, January 23.

McCord, Hugo (1995), "What is the Soul?," *Vigil*, 23[11]:87-88, November.

McGarvey, J.W. (1875), *Commentary on Matthew-Mark* (Delight, AR: Gospel Light), reprint.

Morey, Robert A. (1984), *Death and the Afterlife* (Minneapolis, MN: Bethany House).

Nielsen, Kai (1973), *Ethics Without God* (London: Pemberton).

Orr, James (1956), "Punishment," *International Standard Bible Encyclopedia*, ed. James Orr (Grand Rapids, MI: Eerdmans), 4:2501-2504.

Otten, Herman J. (1988), *Baal or God?* (New Haven, MO: Christian News Publications), revised edition.

Peterson, Robert A. (1995), *Hell on Trial—the Case for Eternal Punishment* (Phillipsburg, NJ: P&R).

Pinnock, Clark (1987), "Fire, Then Nothing," *Christianity Today*, March 20.

Rice, Tim (1987), "Is Hell Eternal in Nature?," *Vigil*, 15[1]:5-6, January.

Robinson, John A.T. (1949), "Universalism—Is It Heretical?," *Scottish Journal of Theology,* June.

Rudin, Norah (1997), *Dictionary of Modern Biology* (Hauppauge, NY: Barrons).

Russell, Bertrand (1967), *Why I am Not a Christian* (New York: Simon & Schuster).

Russell, Bertrand (1969), *Autobiography* (New York: Simon & Schuster).

Sartre, Jean Paul, (1961), "Existentialism and Humanism," *French Philosophers from Descartes to Sartre*, ed. Leonard M. Marsak (New York: Meridian).

Sartre, Jean Paul (1966), "Existentialism," Reprinted in *A Casebook on Existentialism*, ed. William V. Spanos (New York: Thomas Y. Crowell).

Sasse, Herman (1964), "*Aion, Aionios,*" *Theological Dictionary of the New Testament*, ed. Gerhard Kittel (Grand Rapids, MI: Eerdmans), 1:208-209.

Schaff, Phillip (1970 reprint), *History of the Christian Church* (Grand Rapids, MI: Eerdmans).

Stevens, David (1991), "The Place of Eternal Punishment," *Therefore Stand*, 7[3]:21-22, March.

Simpson, George Gaylord (1951), *The Meaning of Evolution* (New York: Mentor).

Smith, F. LaGard (1988), *A Christian Response to the New Age Movement*, Audio taped lecture presented at Pepperdine University, Malibu, California.

Stacey, John (1977), *Sermons on Heaven and Hell* (Rutherford, TN: Stacey Publications).

Taylor, A.E. (1945), *Does God Exist?* (London: Macmillan).

Taylor, Robert R. Jr. (1985), *Challenging Dangers of Modern Versions* (Ripley, TN: Taylor Publications).

Thayer, J.H. (1958 reprint), *A Greek-English Lexicon of the New Testament* (Edinburgh: T. & T. Clark).

Thiele, Gilbert (1958), "Easter Hope," *The Seminarian*, March.

Thompson, Bert (1995a), "The Case for the Existence of God—[Part I]," *Reason and Revelation*, 15:33-38, May.

Thompson, Bert (1995b), "The Case for the Existence of God—[Part II]," *Reason and Revelation*, 15:41-47, June.

Thompson, Bert and Wayne Jackson (1982), "The Revelation of God in Nature," *Reason and Revelation*, 2:17-24, May.

Thompson, Bert and Wayne Jackson (1992), *A Study Course in Christian Evidences* (Montgomery, AL: Apologetics Press).

Vincent, M.R. (1946), *Word Studies in the New Testament* (Grand Rapids, MI: Eerdmans).

Vine, W.E. (1966), *An Expository Dictionary of New Testament Words* (Westwood, NJ: Revell).

Vine, W.E. (1991), *Amplified Expository Dictionary of New Testament Words* (Iowa Falls, IA: World).

Vos, Geerhardus (1956), "Gehenna," *International Standard Bible Encyclopedia*, ed. James Orr (Grand Rapids, MI: Eerdmans), 2:1183.

Wallace, Robert A. (1975), *Biology: The World of Life* (Pacific Palisades, CA: Goodyear).

Warren, Thomas B. (1992), *Immortality—All of Us Will be Somewhere Forever* (Moore, OK: National Christian Press).

Whitelaw, Robert L. (1991), *Can There be Eternal Life Apart from Christ?* (Sterling, VA: GAM Publications).

Woods, Guy N. (1980), "What is the Difference Between the Soul and the Spirit of Man?," *Gospel Advocate*, 122[6]:163, March 20.

Woods, Guy N. (1985), "Do the Scriptures Teach that the Wicked are to Experience Endless Suffering in Hell?," *Gospel Advocate*, 127[9]:278, May 2.

Woods, Guy N. (1985), "What is the Soul of Man?," *Gospel Advocate*, 127[22]:691-692, November 21.

Woodson, Leslie (1973), *Hell and Salvation* (Old Tappan, NJ: Revell).

Workman, Gary (1992), "Is There An Eternal Hell?," *Spiritual Sword*, 23[3]:30-34, April.

Workman, Gary (1993), "Will the Wicked Be Eternally Punished or Annihilated?," *Whatever Happened to Heaven and Hell?*, ed. Terry E. Hightower (San Antonio, TX: Shenandoah Church of Christ), pp. 495-503.

Young, Edward J. (1965), *Psalm 139* (London: The Banner of Truth Trust).

Zerr, E.M. (1952), *Bible Commentary* (Bowling Green, KY: Guardian of Truth Foundation).